HISTORICAL GUIDE TO ANURADHAPURA'S RUINS

HISTORICAL GUIDE TO ANURADHAPURA'S RUINS

H. E. WEERASOORIYA

GYAN

Published by

Gyan Publishing House
5, Ansari Road
Daryaganj, New Delhi-110002
Phone: 011-47034999, 9811692060
E-mail: books@gyanbooks.com

Distribution Network
gyanbooks.com
India, USA, Canada, UK, Australia, France

ISBN : 978-81-212-3493-1 (PB)
First Published, Colombo

2nd Impression 2020

Printed at: Gyan Press, Delhi.

Historical Guide to Anuradhapura's Ruins
Author: H. E. Weerasooriya

Historical Guide

To

Anuradhapura's Ruins

BY

H. E. WEERASOORIYA

W. E. BASTIAN & Co.

NORRIS ROAD, COLOMBO.

TO

RICHMOND

PREFACE.

ON my first visit to Anuradhapura some years ago, when I tried to learn something about the history of these sacred ruins, the general lack of knowledge about them surprised me. I found that what the local residents knew was limited to legends, while the learned priests, perhaps owing to a want of time for a detailed study, had a weakness to fix names from the *Mahawansa* onto these ruined structures, with little facts to support them ; the licenced guides were generally more loquacious than accurate, and the usual kind of guide books merely touched the fringe of the subject. So I decided to study these ruins.

This little book is the outcome of such study. Herein I have tried to bridge the wide gulf that exists between the popular tourists' guide, and the more detailed and specialised work on the subject.

The book takes the form of seven excursions, each commencing at the sacred Bo tree. The last journey takes the visitor to Mihintale, which, as it cannot be completely explored in a single day, has been treated with less detail than the rest. I have included a short sketch of the history of Anuradhapura, which may be skipped over if desired without much detriment to the subject, as I have indicated the ages of the ruins in their respective places.

I have to thank Yatigammana Wimalajnana, Sthavira, Vice-Principal of Anuradhapura Maha Vihare Pirivena, for his kind criticism, and Mr. T. Mendis, Principal of Mahinda College, Anuradhapura, and Mr. C. P. de Alwis, for their valuable help in various ways. My thanks are also due to Mr. W. D. E. Bastian of Messrs. W. E. Bastian & Co., for the help he gave me in securing the illustrations.

I venture to hope that this book will supply the long felt need for a complete and popular work on the ruins of Anuradhapura.

HUBERT E. WEERASOORIYA

Green Path,
Anuradhapura, Ceylon.
November, 1939.

CONTENTS

ILLUSTRATIONS.

ANURADHAPURA

THE history of Anuradhapura begins with the defeat of eight sons of King Panduwasu Dewa in the fifth century B.C. by Pandukabhaya, the great-grand nephew of the first Sinhalese King of Lanka. He had battled with his eight uncles for seventeen years, and after killing them all he entered Anuradhapura, then only a village by the bank of the Kadamba river now called the Malwatu Oya, and made it his capital.

For this information as well as for the rest of the history of Ceylon, we are indebted to that one-thousand-five-hundred year old book, the *Mahawansa*. Mr. James Ferguson in his 'History of Indian and Eastern Architecture' writes, "It alone of all known countries contains a complete series of Buddhist monuments extending from the time of Asoka to the present day, and in the *Mahawansa*, it alone possesses a history so detailed and authentic, that the dates and purposes of the earlier buildings can be ascertained with very tolerable precision."

King Pandukabhaya and his son Mutasiva together ruled for 130 years according to the *Mahawansa*, during which Anuradhapura grew from a village with a handful of men into a densely populated city nearly equalling the size of modern London, having a scavenging force alone of five-hundred to keep clean the broad well planned streets. In addition it had a large reservoir having a surface area of 250 acres, a public cemetery called the 'Great Cemetery' and two large pleasure gardens or parks.

During the reign of the next king, Devanampiya Tissa, the country underwent a tremendous upheaval in the shape of the introduction of Buddhism, and moulded this warlike Aryan tribe from India, into a nation with an ideal to strive for and a spiritual treasure to safeguard even to the bitter end.

The royal *Arahat* or Elder, Mahinda, the son of the Emperor Asoka, of India was the missionary. He is said to have travelled through the air and alighted on the summit of the Mihintale Hill where he met the king who had gone hunting, and then and there converted him.

During this period art grew and flourished side by side with religion. The sacred Bo tree made its historic passage to Ceylon. Beautiful *dagabas* and ornamental ponds and monasteries were built. And a spectacular reservior having more than twice the capacity of the first was also constructed.

Buddhism had a slight drawback during the early part of the second century B.C. when a Tamil invader from the Chola country, called Elara, seized the crown. But he was a just and good ruler and the people did not suffer.

He was defeated and killed by that mighty king from the south, King Dutugemunu, who has now become almost a legendary figure. Dutugemunu's historical fight with Elara. his defeat of the Tamil king in single combat and his wonderful chivalrous respect to his fallen foe, have been immortalised in plays and books by Sinhalese authors throughout the ages.

An ardent supporter of Buddhism and a good friend of the priests, he had a happy weakness for the spectacular. He built magnificent monasteries, gorgeous palaces some nine storeys high, and lofty, golden-pinnacled *dagabas* with their white domes shining in the sun and visible for miles around. To his immortal name will go down for ever the dazzling structures of the Brazen Palace and the Ruwanweli Dagaba.

In his time Anuradhapura reached the zenith of its glory. The people were prosperous and happy; the priests were united for schisms had yet to appear; and no foreign foe had ruthlessly raped the virgin beauty of chaste Anuradhapura, as was done later.

In all ninety-nine kings both friends and foes of the country reigned at Anuradhapura without a break, some only a few days while others ruled as much as sixty years.

A few outstanding names spring to the mind. King Vatta Ghamini Abhaya who ruled during the early part of the first century B.C., built the grand Abhayagiri Dagaba for the sake of revenging himself on a priest of the Jain sect. It was also during this time the first dissension among the priesthood occurred, and the Dhammaruci sect as apart from the Theravada, was formed. Because of this the Buddhist scriptures which had been so far handed down by word of mouth was then taken down in writing.

That most amazing queen, Anula, ruled Anuradhapura towards the middle of the first century B.C. It is interesting to note that so early as then, women held equality of rank in Ceylon.

But still more interesting is her private life which completely left Hollywood in the shade. She had no less than five husbands during the short period of five years, every one of whom she poisoned, and then lived licentiously with thirty two paramours during the remaining four years of her life.

She was killed by Kuttakanna Tissa who built a wall round Anuradhapura, and also constructed a stone *dagaba* at Mihintale, probably the Katu Saeya.

King Bhatikabhaya who followed him had a weakness for novelty. He caused Ruwanweli Dagaba to be buried in a mountain of Jasmine flowers.

King Gaja Bahu, literally Elephant Arm, who reigned in the early part of the second century is said to have invaded India and brought twenty-four thousand captives.

King Voharika Tissa who reigned a century later was a great lawer. He purified the judicial system and removed abuses which had crept into it.

An extreme case of royal piety was witnessed during the reign of King Siri Sanga Bo in the third century. As such he was a misfit as a king. It is during his period that we first hear of 'Bali' ceremonies to drive away sickness.

Mahasena, the great tank-builder and the inveterate enemy of the Maha Vihare sect of priests, reigned during the end of the third century. He wrecked and cruelly tore down all the beautiful monasteries of the Theravada priests and ransacked their treasures. Later he was reconciled to them, but again evoked their disapproval by building the huge *dagaba*, Jetawanarama, in the precincts of the Maha Vihare. Several beautiful monasteries among the Abhayagiri ruins are attributed to him.

He is however better known as the creator of the gigantic reservoir Minneri Wewa in the Tamankaduwa district, and is to this day worshipped as the Minneri god. With him the first part of the *Mahawansa* comes to a close.

The Tooth Relic was conveyed to Ceylon during the reign of the next king, Siri Megawanna, and soon after during the latter half of the fourth century, King Buddhadasa the famous royal physician took up the reins of government. Many are the stories related in the *Mahawansa* about the cures performed by him. He provided dispensaries throughout the Island and placed a physician in charge of every ten villages, a system which in certain interior places exists to this day.

Some lean years followed when foreign rule crushed the people. But they were soon freed from the tyranny by King Dhatusena who drove away the Tamil foes.

King Dhatusena is specially known for the construction of the enormous reservoir Kala Wewa in the fifth century. Kala Wewa to this day replenishes the water supply of Anuradhapura by a giant channel over fifty miles long, the wonderful levels of which are a cause for marvel to engineers of even the present day.

It was King Dhatusena's uncle, the priest Mahanama who wrote the *Mahawansa*. King Dhatusena's notorious son, the parricide Kassappa, then removed the seat of Government to the impenetrable rock-fortress Sigiriya, but his brother Moggallana re-established Anuradhapura as the royal capital.

From thence onwards the star of Anuradhapura began to wane. With increasing trouble at home and constant invasions from abroad, the seventh, eighth and ninth centuries witnessed the decline and fall of Anuradhapura, till finally towards the end of the ninth century this royal city was deserted and Polonnaruwa became the capital. The impressive and brilliant spectacle that was Anuradhapura was no more. Instead desolateness reigned. And the jungle tide ever advancing soon reclaimed its own. The glory of Anuradhapura had departed

Today excavated Anuradhapura allows us to get a glimpse of its wonderful past. As we gaze on the massive remains of the buildings, especially the *dagabas* and tanks, as the artistic and elaborate ornamentations in relief stare at us from every side, and the gorgeous and splendid moon-stones, those dreams in granite, irresistibly draw us to them, our minds fly back to two-thousand years. And as from this maze of cut and carved stones we reconstruct vivid pictures of temples and lands, of monasteries, *dagabas*, gardens and parks, of hospitals, granaries and store-houses, of channels and aqueducts, for a brief second we are enabled to recapture the ancient glory of old Anuradhapura.

FIRST EXCURSION

THERE is no fitter place to start the tour of the ruins of Anuradhapura than at the sacred Bo tree, the proudest possession of Lanka. It was brought to Ceylon in the middle of the third century B.C. during the reign of King Devanampiya Tissa amid much glory and splendour, devotion and delight, for it was a branch of the actual Bo tree under which Gautama attained Buddhahood. The *Mahawansa* becomes extravagantly lyrical about its arrival in Ceylon, and many are the miracles supposed to have happened during its historical journey from India.

The day it arrived at Anuradhapura, the Holy City was bedecked like a bride to receive her groom. It was evening. The capital was superbly decorated. White sand was strewn on the streets and covered with *pavada* or glistening white carpets. Banners hung above. The people dressed in their best with joyful piety thronged the sides as the majestic elephants swaying from side to side, conscious of the greatness of the occasion, and resplendent in all their glory, heralded the advent of this treasure.

Thus was brought this living monument of Buddhism which has lived through times of prosperity, trials and tribulations, and has keenly associated itself with the growth and the fall of the Sinhalese nation. And today, it still lives silvery with age, the oldest authenticated tree in the world.

The visitor sees a rather uncouthly walled quadrangle of granite blocks which at first sight seems to guard a miniature forest of bo trees. Entering it through a picturesque gateway a paved path leads through an avenue of bo trees to a higher bank of terraced earth. Just before ascending this terrace the attention is attracted by a huge standing statue of Buddha, in a blessing attitude. It was found buried right up to the *Sirespotha* or conventionalised halo on the head. It is a great pity that it is most unimaginatively white washed ! Two more ancient stone Buddhas were discovered on this spot, but these too have been painted over. They are to be seen in the new image-houses.

Ascending a second terrace by a flight of steps, the sacred Bo tree itself is disclosed up above, on a third walled square, safely enclosed by a protective railing of bronze. It looks weak and fragile as it stands surrounded by giant bo trees three to four times as big. But its wonderful dignity as it surveys the world, leaning on its bronze staffs, is amazing.

In front of this enclosure stands one thousand six hundred towering granite pillars. This is the ruin of the famous nine-storeyed Lowa Maha Paya or the Brazen Palace, built by the warrior king Dutugemunu two-thousand years ago and gifted to the priests. Even today there is not a single building in Ceylon which has even eight storeys. Ceylon had sky-scrapers long before America was even discovered.

The upper portion which was of wood-work has completely perished, and there is nothing to indicate what the building must have looked like in the time of its glory.

The *Mahawansa* describes its greatness and splendour graphically, and concludes :—" This edifice surrounded by a highly polished wall, and having four embattled gates, shone forth like the Vejavanta Palace in the Tavatinsa heavens. This building was covered with brazen tiles: hence it acquired the appellation of the 'Brazen Palace' " It must indeed have been a remarkable structure.

The road that runs north of the Bo tree absolutely follows the course of the ancient street, and is appropriately called the Sacred Road. The older residents call it the Maha Chandra Wanka Weediya, an ancient street which proceeded on to Mihintale.

Deviating a little from this road a spacious ruin near the present Post Office discloses a picturesque *jantaghara* or hot water bathing-place. Here is seen for the first time a so-called granite 'Conjee boat'! This was actually the receptacle for holding water.

Back to the road and it leads us to an array of pillars in front of Ruwanweli Seya, which mark an unusual ruin. Here are four cylindrical pillars around a granite table, the only cylindrical pillars to be found at Anuradhapura.

Just behind this structure is a *kesakutiya gala* or closet stone, by far the finest bit of sculpture in its own line. For sheer skill of execution and perfection of workmanship this bit of work is hard to beat. Surrounding this, is a ruin with two rows of several little cells. Mr. Bell, the then Archaelogical Commissioner, called it a *Parivena* or a place where priests dwelt. The local residents believe it to be the site of an ancient hospital, for the fact must not be forgotten that the priests were then, as in some places even now, the ministers of the body as well as the soul.

Only two such identical buildings have been found at Anuradhapura, the other one being by the side of the Thuparama. In front of both these were discovered and are to be seen today what look like granite coffins or sarcophagi. Only three such coffins have been found in the Holy City, the third being to the west of the Kali Kovil.

Some explain their presence near these ruins by suggesting that they were used as 'milk baths' to extract the poison from snake bites. While in the state of coma produced by a snake bite the patient was supposed to have been lowered into the sarcophagus and covered with milk into which had been added the juice of poison-extracting herbs.

But the interior measurements of these sarcophagi seem to be too individual in character to be used for such a general purpose. Instead, from the *Mahawansa* we learn that when great personages died they were not buried immediately but were embalmed and kept for seven days, so that the public could pay their respects. This was so done in the case of *Arahat* Mahinda and the *Theri* Sanghamitta, the Arahat's sister. And it is more probable to suppose that these sarcophagi were used to keep the embalmed bodies for public view. Perhaps this ruin enclosing the granite table within the four cylindrical posts marks the funeral hall mentioned in the *Mahawansa*, as the place where the *Arahat* Mahinda's corpse was kept embalmed for seven days. It was thereafter known as *Pangnambamalaka*.

To the right of these ruins, the remains of a monastery can be seen. To the south of this monastery a lane leads into a greeny glade, in which stands in poetic loneliness a little brick built *dagaba* styled Sela Cheitiya, or Stone Dagaba,—an absolute contradiction. Of the Sela Cheitiya, the *Mahawansa* definitely says that it was in front of the Thuparama, while *Dipawansa*, another ancient chronicle, puts it down as on " the east of the Thuparama." The only *dagaba* which corresponds to both these is the so-called Sanghamitta Dagaba.

The local priests call this *dagaba* the Kujji Tissa Vehera, Kujji Tissa being an ancient *arahat.* His relics are supposed to be enshrined in it.

The Sacred Road leads us along a row of modern Government bungalows which have been instrumental in the ruthless destruction and spoliation of the series of fine monasteries that ranged the eastern side of the Ruwanweli Seva.

Nearing the Government hospital, the ancient Maha Mega pleasure gardens are left behind, and we cross on to the Nandana pleasure gardens.

In front of the hospital is a large, filled up pond with a grass grown mound on the fringe of it. The people call this pond the 'Kuruwe wewa' or Elephant pond. It is possibly the pond which the royal elephant of King Devanampiya Tissa was wont to frequent, and by the edge of which on this account the king built a *dagaba* enshrining a relic. The Hatthalahka nunnery was built close to it which subsequently became the chief nunnery of the *Theri* Sanghamitta. As though confirming it an artistic example of a rectangular stone trough close by is called the Elephant's Trough.

A little way along Inner Circular Road and a grass grown mound disclosing a small *dagaba*, is seen. This has not been identified. It was dug into by Mr. Bell, but no relic chamber was discovered. However, an unusual object was found among the debris in the shape of a human skull with a jaw bone containing exceptionally large teeth. This was once more buried; enshrined in a modern cement-built relic, chamber in the same ruin.

In front of this is an *awasa* or monk's residence, which must have been of more than one storey. Just bordering this is another ancient street about thirty-five feet wide, commencing from the Ruwanweli Seya and running parallel to the Sacred Road. It is rather surprising to note that even two-thousand years ago, roads were built far wider than most thoroughfares of today.

Facing this street is the guard-room of the walled precincts of the Thuparama Dagaba. By the side of the guard-house is a shallow roughly -hewn granite receptacle for holding water These are usually found placed outside the monasteries and *vihares* to enable the worshippers to wash their hands and feet before entering the sacred enclosure.

This *dagaba* the first to be built in Ceylon, was caused by King Devanampiya Tissa two-thousand years ago! In it is enshrined the right collar bone of Buddha. The three rows of slender granite pillars which surround this recently reconstructed *dagaba*, now looking piteously out of place, then held a canopy. The friezes of lions and dwarfs adorning the tenons of the pillars are exceedingly beautiful and artistic.

Dagabas, literally relic-tombs, were first built by Egyptians in pyramidical shape while in the East the structure assumed the form of a solid dome. Pre-Buddhist Phoenician tombs were of this shape and it is possible that this was copied by the east, especially Ceylon, where soon the genius of the Sinhalese craftsmen evolved the present artistic shape, suitable to the inborn aesthetic sense of the people.

The *dagaba* in its simplest form is a hemispherical brick or mud built construction resting on three consecutive rings as at Lankarama, or three basal ledges as at Ruwanweli Seya. A square tee surmounts this, and it is here mostly, the relics were enshrined. A short cylinder called the *devata kotuwa* or gods enclosure rises above this, and a spiral cone surmounts the *devata kotuwa*. On the topmost portion of the spire stood a golden or metal pinnacle called the *kota*. In older ones a *chatta* or umbrella of gold guarded the jewels on the *kota* from the elements. Sometimes this *chatta* was pierced by the *kota*.

In front of the *dagaba* is another beautiful stone vessel, similar to the granite 'Elephant's Trough.' These troughs served the same purpose as *Pin-taliyas* do today, namely to keep water for those thirsty to drink. This idea is strengthened by the fact that these troughs are found even in the city proper, as apart from the sacred precincts, thereby dis-associating themselves from anything pertaining to sacred places alone.

On the south-east of the Thuparama Dagaba is a building built by King Devanampiya Tissa at about the same time as the *dagaba*, and when the Tooth Relic was brought to Ceylon, six-hundred years later, used as the *Dalada Maligawa* or Tooth Relic Palace. This is a unique building, four of its inner pillars having elongated capitals representing conventionalised lotus buds, and the innermost four, highly polished, —a rare occurrence among the ruins at Anuradhapura.

Here is found a fine example of a *sandakada pahana* or moon-stone, a highly artistic form of door-step. The moon-stones form some of the cleverest and most beautiful sculptures found at Anuradhapura.

By the side of this ruin is a good example of an ancient well, its sides formed of dressed slabs of granite, not one out of place.

On the east of the *dagaba* is the so-called Sanghamitta Thupa, very probably the real Sela Cheitiya Dagaba. According to the *Mahawansa* the *Theri* was cremated on the spot between the Thuparama and the bo tree which was one of the eight original shoots of the sacred Bo tree. The ashes were collected and a *dagaba* built on the spot where she was cremated. Thus, this spot must be on the west of the Thuparama. No sign of it now remains.

On the north of the Thuparama is an ancient pond now in sad ruin. These ponds which dotted the compounds of the monasteries were fed by the Abhaya Wewa by connected channels.

On the south of the Thuparama a whole series of monasteries stretch in echeleon order right up to Ruwanweli Seya. The monastery in which the monks of the Thuparama dwelt is just by the south boundary of the *dagaba* precincts. It must have been a very important monastery judging by the remains of the chief residence of the priests. The solid granite pillars still remaining intact convey the impression of a spectacular building of several storeys. The stone coffin-shaped vessel by its side has sometimes misled observers to believe the structure to be an ancient hospital. A clever example of a *kesakutiya gala or* closet-stone is observable behind the row of cells on the south of the structure.

A striking and singular building is come across on the way to Ruwanweli Seya from Thuparama. At first it must have been a palace as evident by the unique specimens of genre carvings adorning the outer faces of its balustrades, and the royal lions on the inner faces. Later it may have been given over to the priesthood. It may even possibly be Princess Anula's palace reported in the *Mahawansa* to have been used as a nunnery of the Hatthalakha priestesses. This view Is strengthened by the massive walls, the proximity of the Elephant's tank, and the fact that it has nearly twelve apartments, which princess Anula's palace too is said to have had.

These monasteries were of a definite plan. In each, in the middle was situated the *Vihare* or image-house, while four monk's residences adorned its four corners. Close to the *awasas* or monk's residences were one or two out-houses such as a closet, identifiable by the artistically carved closet-stone. A bathing pond completed the unit.

There were, however, more elaborate monasteries of single factions such as the one at Puliyankulama where there were as much as thirty-two *awasas* to a single monastery.

Ruwanweli Seya ! The most venerated and mightiest of the *dagabas*, it is bigger than the third pyramid at Gizeh in Egypt both in contents and height !

The *Arahat* Mahinda informed King Devanampiya Tissa that this was a place consecrated by all four Buddhas, and that in time to come a *dagaba* would be built here one-hundred-and-twenty cubits high to enshrine relics of Gautama Buddha. The king hearing this was anxious to proceed with the ambitious work himself but the *Arahat* stayed him, and foretold that one of his descendants named Duttha Ghamini Abhaya, six generations, later would be the one to construct the *dagaba*. Thereupon, the king caused this prophecy to be engraved on a stone pillar and put up at the spot. This pillar exists to this day on the northern side of the *dagaba*; but the inscription is completely worn out.

King Dutugemunu ultimately fulfilled this prophecy and built the spectacular *dagaba* referred to in the histories at various times as the Maha Thupa, Hemamali, Suwarnamali and Ratnamali. At that time it was the grandest structure in the city, and with its great white dome visible for miles around glistening in the sun, bid fair to lessen the splendour of even the Brazen Palace.

There is a beautiful story in the *Mahawansa* that the king was not able to complete the *dagaba* before his death. The king's brother however, in order not to disappoint the dying monarch, caused a skeleton structure to be put up by means of bamboos, and covered it with white cloth to represent the *dagaba* as it would look when completed. And the monarch was pleased, and while gazing at it expired.

The outer *dagaba*, according to the ancient chronicles, is built over two other *dagabas*, one within the other. That it at least encloses one is certified by Mr. Parker, in his 'Ancient Ceylon', which records that while the *dagaba* was being cleared of the debris, part of the brick work slipped down, disclosing a second structure within. Of this *dagaba* the same writer remarks, "It was a striking memorial of its great founder and of the artistic genius of the Sinhalese race." Its glory is further vividly and lavishly described in the *Mahawansa*.

By its side is a miniature, a facsimile of the Ruwanweli Seya carved out of a single slab of a kind of lime stone, a rare work of art. Some believe that this was the model constructed and approved by the king before the actual work was begun. In this connection there is an interesting story. The king inquired from the chosen architect in what form the *dagaba* would be built. Thereupon the builder took some water in a golden dish and dashed another handful of water onto it. A great globule like a ball of crystal rose to the surface, and he pointing it to the king informed him that he would construct it in that shape. The monarch was delighted and bestowed on him " a suit of clothes worth a thousand, and a pair of slippers and twelve-thousand Kahapanas." On this Mr. Parker cynically comments that 'at the present day even the slippers are not given to successful architects in Ceylon.! '

Others believe that this tiny *dagaba* does not represent a model constructed before Ruwanweli Seya was built, but is probably the miniature that was caused in the twelth century by King Nissanka Malla, as reported in the *Mahawansa*.

The kings who followed tried to outbeat each other in their benefactions and gifts to the 'Great Dagaba.'

Of these, King Bhaṭikabhaya who reigned about the time of Christ, caused the whole *dagaba* to be buried in a mound of Jasmine flowers, and then "raising water from the Abhaya Wewa by means of machinery" caused the flowers to be sprayed. This king is said to have had an earnest longing to see the gorgeous relic-chamber described in the *Mahawansa*, as having been built by Dutugemunu. And with that idea fixed in his head he lay himself down on the south-east side of the *dagaba* and refused to rise till he had beheld its glory. The *Mahawansa* reports that the priests caused a passage to open itself and the king was taken and shown the relic-chamber. The granite figure found towards the south of the *dagaba* is said to be that of Bhatikabhaya.

Two other statues on the east of the *dagaba* are pointed out as those of King Dutugemunu and his illustrious mother, Vihara Maha Devi. Five statues discovered buried in the compound and now housed in the modern image-house are said to be those of the five Buddhas of this era including Maitree Buddha who is still to come.

An upright granite tablet bears an inscription of King Nissanka Malla, who visited the *dagaba* in the twelth century, and describes his offerings to the *dagaba* and the repairs he caused to the Mirisaveṭiya. The huge flower-alters surrounding the *dagaba* are very attractive and artistic, and the *wahalkadas* or cornices with friezes of elephant's heads are a treat to the eyes. On some of the ruined figures of brick-built elephant heads surrounding the parapet of the stone-paved courtyard, the old ornamentations still remain giving an indication of the grand appearance it must have presented.

On the courtyard of the *maluwa* are to be seen pieces of a tall granite pillar, probably used to strengthen the spire, like the one recently found at Polonnaruwa.

The *dagaba* is being rebuilt. But as with each sweep of the brush some wonderful feature is hidden beneath the coating of white, it seems to us to disconnect itself more and more from those glorious days of old. It no longer touches our hearts as does the tragic sight of the other two gigantic *dagabas*.

To the west of the Ruwanweli Seya the series of monasteries, each separated from one another by walls, extend up to the bund of Abhaya Wewa. From amidst this array of stone buildings, two structures stand out like granite Buddhas among Hindu gods. For sheer skill of execution of the moon-stones which grace the steps, and the stone balustrades with the life-like Naga guardian-stones, they are unsurpassable; while the friezes carved on the artistic capitals are hard to beat.

Miscalled 'pavilions', they are actually Uposatha Halls consecrated for worship, and for performing the functions of the priesthood. There are only six of these in the whole of Anuradhapura. Just by Abhaya Wewa on the west of these halls is a little hillock. This has not been identified, though some think that it was the place where the machinery for drawing water to spray the Ruwanweli Seya, after having buried it in a mountainous heap of Jasmine flowers by King Bhatikabhaya, was fixed. Others believe it to be the ruin of a terraced image-house similar to the ones at Toluwila and Puliyankulama.

The large reservoir covering some 250 acres, the Abhaya Wewa, functions as well as ever, the oldest tank in repair in the Island. It is a century older than the sacred Bo tree.

To the south-west of the hillock, close to the Office Assistant's bungalow, are four more monasteries on either side of a broad street which ran west. Most of the stone pillars have disappeared, probably to supply material for the modern buildings close to it. Evidence of a *Wata-da-ge*, a small *dagaba* in a kind of image-house, as well as a rough mound, probably another unidentified *dagaba*, are to be seen.

The monasteries on the compound of the Government Agent's residence have met the same fate.

To the south-east of the Court House is a brick ruin popularly supposed to mark the tomb of King Dutugemunu. It is however only the site of an ancient Kovil.

Along Kachcheri road are the ruins of two bathing ponds, one in a perfect state of preservation while the other is in complete ruin. This pond formed one of the *Atamasthane* or Eight-sacred-places. having been blessed by the *Arahat* Mahinda. This forms one of the most exquisite ruins in the whole of Anuradhapura.

SECOND EXCURSION

THE sacred Bo tree was said to have been planted in front of the King's palace. The palace would naturally have been facing east, for even today, where possible, houses are seldom built except facing the rising sun. Thus the palace very likely stood on the west of the Bo tree, and its site must have occupied the area now covered by the hundreds of shops and boutiques which range the sides of the Main Street and the Kurunegala Road. And it adds no consolation to think that the very stones of the royal palace must have been ruthlessly pulled out and broken to build the eye-sores that line these roads. Perhaps its foundations lie no more than two or three feet below the surface.

A few yards along Kurunegala Road, on the north of the old palace-site, and the so-called Peacocks Palace comes into view. This stands on one of the Eight-sacred-places blessed by *Arahat* Mahinda, and from what he uttered then we learn the uses of these beautiful and unusual structures. The *Mahawansa* gives it lucidly :—

" . . . . . . on this spot the Malaka had stood; now also it wll become to the Priesthood the place where their rites and ceremonies will be performed."

A little further on, and a grass-grown tree-covered mound with the side facing the road burrowed into like a rat-eaten loaf of bread, is seen by the road side. This was popularly supposed to be the tomb of the Tamil King Elara, until Mr. Bell excavated it and definitely proved it to be a *dagaba*, the Dakkina Thupa or Southern Dagaba built by Uttiya, one of the eight warriors of King Watta Ghamini Abhaya in the first century B.C. How this glaring mistake came about is explained in this way by the older residents of the town.

When Anuradhapura was being excavated, all the Indian conservancy coolies and other Tamil labourers settled down in this part of the city, and owing to a lack of better facilitics began to use this jungle-covered mound for purposes far from religious. To stop this sacrilege, an intelligent Buddhist spread the rumour that it was the very tomb of their renowned King Elara that they were desecrating. This news soon got round and the dirty practice quickly came to an end. But though it attained its purpose the misnomer remained !

A quarter of a mile more, and the turning to Isurumuniya is passed. A further mile forward, and we become lost in a collection of mighty boulders, caves, bricks, pillars, ponds and ruins of all descriptions.

This is Vessagiriya, literally the rock shelters of the commoners. The *Arahat* Mahinda having ordained five-hundred princes into the priest-hood at Isurumuniya, came hither and ordained five-hundred *vaisyas* or commoners. Hence it was called Vaisya-giri which became Vessagiri.

Some of the best specimens of Veddah caves are to be seen here. For, there is little doubt that years before the monks took charge of the caves they were used by the Veddahs, the forest dwellers of Ceylon. Over these caves *kataras* or drip-ledges have been cut to lead away the rain water. Along many of these drip-ledges inscriptions are to be seen, marking the name of the donors of these caves to the priests.

The smoothened rock-beds where the *Arahats* slept can be observed on the granite surfaces inside the caves. How the caves were walled in is disclosed by the structure of the cave in which a granite door still stands attached to the stark rock, by a solid brick wall.

Close to this granite doorway is an inscription which reads, "Isuru-Meni-Bo-Ipuluwan-Kasumbagiri-Vihare." This links Vessagiriya with Sigiriya of the parricide Kassyapa fame.

Kassyapa or Kasumba, later repented of his ghastly act and tried by deeds of great merit to smoothen away the wickedness of his crime. The *Mahawansa* tells us that he gifted innumerable lands to Isurumuniya and Vessagiriya and he built a monastery and called it after the names of his two daughters, Bo, Ipuluwan, and himself, Kasumba.

The foundations of a small *dagaba* are to be seen on the top of one of the rocks. Some of the walls of brick-structures still remain on the rocky foundations, while the plaster laid two-thousand years ago exists in patches even to this day.

Here too, several monasteries are traceable, most of them being of the familiar quincunx group of image-house and four *awasas* or monks' residences. That the rocks to the furthest south have been quarried to supply the major portion of the granite pillars needed for the myriads of sacred buildings at Anuradhapura, is seen by the evidence of the many marks of the stone workers so vividly left behind. Here is a stone pillar split and ready for transport; another with all the necessary holes drilled in the stone and only the word needed for the hammers to fall in unison and split it; a third, half drilled, and at a fourth rock only the outline marked. And it is as well to remember that this method of splitting stones was known in England only in the nineteenth century, a method which had been raised to an art in Ceylon two-thousand years earlier !

Back along Kurunegala Road onto Isurumuniya, the place where the *Arahat* Mahinda first ordained five-hundred *issaras* or royal princes, because of which it was called 'Issara Samanaramaya,' which translated to Sinhalese became Isurumuniya.

To the archaeological student Isurumuniya is a treasure trove, while to the interested visitor it is a place of indefinable charm. Towards the centre of this towering rock a square chamber is hewn out of the living granite, having on its doorway a remarkable relief of a *Makara Torana*, the arch of the fabulous Buddhist monster. The workmanship of that delicate carving is superb. Only a master-craftsman's hands could have executed it.

Inside the chamber a granite Buddha carved out of the same rock meditates among scented offerings, with that inscrutable smile hovering round the unchanging lips. On the immediate right of the rock-cut chamber, a figure of a seated equestrian carved in relief with a horse's head peering over his right shoulder has puzzled many an archaeologist. This has no significance with Buddhism. And neither has the carving on the left of the chamber, a sculpture in relief of a man and a woman in a unique love-making scene, the woman being seated on the lap of the man. Is this the Hindu god Aiyanaar and his wife Skanda, still held in great esteem by the Wanni or jungle folk of Ceylon? Or could it be the all powerful Ishwara with his mate ?

Various theories have been propounded about these carvings by archaeologists, and they have come to the conclusion that Isurumuniya before it was turned to a Buddhist monastery was a religious institution of whatever pre-Buddhist religion that existed in Ceylon, probably a form of Jainism, and that these figures were connected with that religion.

On the south of the chamber, the rock dips into a picturesque pond. From the water level several carved elephants stand on the rock surface in low relief with their trunks all pointing to a gaping hole of about two feet square, which must have contained some valuable articles subsequently rifled.

On the south of the chamber a new image-house is being built, enclosing the cave where the *Arahat* Mahinda reposed. Even though it may not appeal to the lover of these ancient ruins, and one may be inclined to dub it a vandalism, it provides the visitor with a diversion to compare the art of the past and the present, here existing literally side by side.

Inside the new image-house, is to be seen the sign of a book carved on the rock. The residents believe that this is a sign to show that the Tri-Pitaka, which contains the teachings of the Buddha, are deposited inside the rock.

A picturesque *dagaba* graces the southern summit of the rock. On the northern end of the summit the imprint of the sacred foot has been recently carved. But the beauty of the rock has been somewhat marred by the unbecoming modern bell-tower built over the rock-cut chamber.

The rock of Isurumuniya laps the bund of Tisa Wewa reservoir. Originally the marshy pond Jaya Vapi, Devanampiya Tissa had it enlarged and constructed the Tisa Wewa by building a mighty embankment across its valley. This substantially built bund is twenty-five to thirty feet high, and two-and-a-half miles long. "The bank" writes Mr. Parker, "is a well made and substantial work which with a little attention may last practically for ever. It appears to be in its original state and is a credit to the man who raised it." At present Tisa Wewa supplies the life-blood of the town in the shape of the drinking water.

Just below the bund and quite close to Isurumuniya are a few boulders, heavily intermingled among which are found a series of ruins. Though they may have later been given over to the priesthood, that at one time they were secular buildings is proved by the delightful bathing ponds attached to them.

These ponds are some of the best preserved and artistic ruins to be found at Anuradhapura, not second to the gorgeous pond along the Kachcheri Road.

There are three ponds in all, and in two of them are bas-reliefs of bathing elephants, a very charming scene. The ponds were filled with water by a triple spout passing from underneath the bund of Tisa Wewa and connected onto the smaller pond, from which the water flowed into the others.

Towards the extreme southern end of these boulders are signs of a very ancient building, among which several shallow caves, some with drip-ledges, are to be observed. On a steeply projecting side of one of the rocks facing the bund, a queer inscription is carved. This inscription has recently been proved to be pre-Buddhist and probably about five-thousand years old! It is in the form of a *chakra*, or circle having a second inner circle, between which there are several signs. The *chakra* has been divided by lines into four equal quadrants, while at the exact centre there are a number of concentric circles.

Of this inscription, that learned Oriental scholar, Mr. W. A. de Silva (the Hon'ble the Minister of Health) writes: "The Yakkas of Ceylon had their own history though hardly any traces of their language and their institutions are seen now, except perhaps an inscription on a stone near Tisa Wewa, at Anuradhapura. . . . . . Professor D. M. Robison in his report on excavations of the city of Olynthus in Macedonia, which locality he estimates was inhabited from over 3000 B.C. gives a diagram of the floor of a house which he names the 'Villa of Good Fortune.' In this diagram are seen a number of signs which bear a resemblance to some of the signs in the diagram at Tisa Wewa inscription."

Along the bund of Tisa Wewa, past the low level sluice, and Puttalam Road is reached. A little way along Puttalam Road, in the direction of the town, the russet coloured Mirisaveti Dagaba breaks into view.

King Dutugemunu in the second century B.C., having conquered his Tamil foe, on the seventh day after the victory held a water festival at the Tisa Wewa; at which he with all his retinue, having deposited their clothes and the royal sceptre a little distance from the tank, sported in the water. After having enjoyed himself, when he made preparations to depart, he found that the sceptre could not be pulled out of the ground. Thereupon the King remembering that one day, contrary to his vow, he had failed to share a chillie pod with the priests' and believing this to be the cause of the strange happening, constructed a *dagaba* over the spot, enshrining the sceptre which held a relic of Buddha, inside it. And he called this *dagaba* 'The Maricca-veti Dagaba' in commemoration of the Maricca or chillie incident. Mariccaveti in Sinhalese became Mirisaveti Dagaba, which it is now called.

Mirisavetiya was the first of the great *dagabas*. Thus the first to appreciate the eloquent grandeur of a sparkling white dome bigger than any of its kind found either in India or Ceylon, was the great King Dutugemunu. This *dagaba* possesses some unique *wahalkadas* or cornices. An attempt to rebuild it was made some fifty years ago at the expense of a Siamese prince, but the work was stopped half-way.

A whole town of monasteries stretch from the precincts of the *dagaba* like undulating waves. The familiar quincunx group has here given place to a unit of three buildings to a monastery. In certain door-slabs, can still be seen the iron lined socket in which the pivot of the door swung.

On the west of the *dagaba* is the chief *awasa*, the counterpart of the chief monks' residences at Jetawanarama and Thuparama. It is easily discernible by the array of square granite columns.

On the south of the *dagaba* is a ruin different from the usual run of image-houses or monks' residences. It is a paved square, and by its side is a rock-hewn receptacle similar to the 'Conjee Boats' but somewhat rectangular in shape. This is also a *jantaghara* or bathing place.

What strikes one very forcibly among these ruins at Anuradhapura are the *Doratupalayas* or guard-stones which decorate the sides of the steps of even the most insignificant buildings. Always carved with a delicacy evoking instant admiration, the figures represented therein varies from athletic looking men with five to nine cobra-heads posing over their head-dresses, to simple flower pots. The figures of the men are those of the Naga race, distinguishable by the cobra-heads found usually over their head-dresses or to a side of their heads.

Hence the Nagas, the original inhabitants who were conquered by the Sinhalese must have been snake worshippers, and a very fierce people. And as such they were probably employed as gate-keepers or guards by the victors, in the same way as Negro porters are employed by white men. Thus gradually they became conventionalised as guards of treasures and sacred places.

Sometimes the ill-formed figure of Bhairawa, the defender of temples and buried treasures and the god of the under-world, adorned the guard-stones, such as the exquisitely ugly pair at Abhayagiri Dagaba. Invariably it meant that heaps of rich treasures had been buried in the vicinity.

The symbol of the flower pot reliefs has however not yet been satisfactorily explained.

THIRD EXCURSION

IN the heart of the modern town of Anuradhapura, in front of the present electric power house, is a solitary and unusual ruin well guarded by an iron railing. The more educated people call it the Ransinamalakaya, having identified it from the ancient chronicles, but with what cause or reason is not known. From what is left of the foundations there is enough evidence to show that once an important and imposing granite-pillard structure stood here. But situated as it is, it had long past met the terrible fate that overtook all those ruins which were unfortunate enough to stand close to roads and residences. No foreign vandals ever wrecked these precious monuments more systematically than those road-constructing pioneers and the early building-contractors.

Along Mihintale road up to the 'Pin Bungalow' no ruins are met. But rounding the bend of the Outer Circular Road a whole beehive of monasteries grouped round the Jetawanarama breaks into view, with that majestic *dagaba* looking forlorn and weary with the weight of years sighing in the distance.

In this area no less than thirteen monasteries have been identified, each within its own boundary wall, and also some extraordinarily unique, solitary ruins.

Perhaps the most striking of them is the one called 'The Buddhist Railing Site.' Here is found a large rectangular building with a stone railing, such as has never been discovered elsewhere in Ceylon. This ruin was completely dug by Mr. Bell, and he finally drew the conclusion that two or even three structures had been built one over the other.

Signs of a small *dagaba* with a broken relic-chamber were discovered within the enclosure. Several Sri Patula or Sacred-Foot stones and pieces of granite Buddhas are to be seen to this day, littered about the centre of this strange ruin. A number of beads and coloured glasses were discovered at this spot adding more to the mystery of what it had been in the prime of its glory. Only one fact is known for a certainty, —that it was copied from the similar and more elaborate stone railings in India, such as those at Buddha Gaya and Sanchi. In its hey-day it must indeed have been a remarkable building.

The most important monastery of the whole entourage and which enclosed the chief residence of the Jetavanarama monks, lies towards the east of the Buddhist Railing. It has the usual entrance or guard-house, an image-house and monks' residences. The chief *awasa* or residence is instantly recognizable by the vast number of pillars and the immense size of the structure. The pillars are about two feet square, but as this structure had the misfortune to lie by the side of the Kandy-Trincomalee Road, there is not one single whole pillar left.

This solid structure is similar to the chief *awasas* attached to the Thuparama and Mirisavetiya monasteries, and it can be safely surmised that it must have had several storeys, for some of the pillars were found sunk thirteen feet into the ground, and further strengthened by brick-work.

To the north of this *awasa*, close to some Government bungalows, lies the chief image-house of the monastery. This was carefully excavated by Mr. Bell and a uniqe feature was brought to light. In all other balustrades siding the door-steps, the artistic carving of the imaginary monster *Makara* was made to face outwards. But in this single instance, the Makaras lie facing inwards grotesquely like crocodiles basking in the sun.

A surprising discovery, which brought pictures of eastern splendour to the imagination, was made when it was noticed that one of the pillars had still attached to it a coating of mica flakes! Had mica lined the inner walls of all the sacred buildings in Ceylon ?

Of this ruin Mr. Bell writes :—" We have no inscription to help us in determining the name and age of this fine building. In the day of its glory it must have presented a magnificent appearance exteriorly, with its mild white basement and stairs of quartz glittering in the sun light; whilst within, after dark, the chaste beauty of the carving at the shrine would be immeasurably enhanced by lights coruscating from columns mica-cased."

On the opposite side of the road is a second image-house on a terraced bank. Here is seen a *Yantra Gala* or Charm Stone with all its twenty-five chambers rifled.

To the north-east of this *pilima-ge* lies another of those beautifully executed Uposatha Halls, probably the one belonging to the Jetavanarama monks. It has somewhat suffered at the hands of stone seekers.

To the north-west of the 'Buddhist Railing' the series of monasteries stretch in echeleon order until they culminate in an exceptional brick-built structure having a towering granite doorway twenty-six feet high ! It is an image-house which once housed a colossal image of Buddha, twenty-eight-and-half feet high! But not a vestige of this gigantic image remains, except the shattered portion of the huge lotus-shaped pedestal on which the stupendous granite sculpture once stood.

The square slabs of stones with twenty-five holes and some with nine which were found among the ruins, for a long time puzzled a great many people. The theory was then advanced that they were 'Yogi Stones' used by the ancient *arahats* in their religious observances and meditations. But when several were discovered underneath the foundations of a monastery at Vijayarama, this theory was dropped. How could meditation stones come to lie at the bottom of foundations. Gradually by circumstantial evidence the exact nature of these stones began to be understood. They were actually relic and treasure chambers, which by the very nature of the substances placed within them served the purpose of charms, usually deposited underneath the *asanayas* or seats of holy statues, or beneath the foundations of sacred buildings, to guard them against evil. Thus the stones acted both as treasure chambers, and charms or potencies against evil. And this was definitely proved to be so when recently, at Polonnaruwa, a *Yantra Gala* was found intact in which were some sacred relics and the gems of the nine kinds,—a *Navaratna*, which the Sinhalese still believe to be a powerful charm against evil.

A few yards to the west of this image-house is the 'Halpanu Ela' a huge channel from ten to twenty feet deep and about twice as broad at the top. It starts some distance up the Malwatu-Oya, the river that flows through Anuradhapura, at a substantial stone weir called the Allekatu and now in ruin, travels through the middle of the Maha Mega garden and falls back to the Malwatu Oya past the town.

When the weir was in order it must have directed a large volume of water into Halpanu Ela, and many have been the conjectures as to its use. Irrigation has been ruled out, as then, when Anuradhapura was the metropolis, there were no paddy fields within a range of several miles of the town. The local people call it the Halpanu Ela or Rice-residue Channel and explain that the water of this channel was used to wash the rice cooked and offered at the Maha Vihare. And there was such an enormous quantity washed daily that the whole channel used to turn a muddy colour! Hence the name.

Mr. Bell believed it to be utilised as a kind of drainage system, all the dirt and residue of the town being led by side drains into this main channel and washed away, thereby assuring the cleanliness of the city.

This theory is somewhat doubtful, for, as the water of the Malwatu Oya was used by towns further down, a conscientious king would not have allowed such contamination. Moreover flowing water was held in great regard by the people as evident by that ancient Sinhalese saying: 'Never despise either flowing water or the mother that gave birth to you.'

Perhaps the truth is that stated in the *Mahawansa*: "In the reign of Senindagutta, (Mittasena in the 5th century,) the Damilas, to ensure the cleanliness which attends bathing, considering the river to be too remote for that purpose, forming an embankment across it, brought it's stream near the town."

The Jetavanarama Dagaba lies to the right of the huge image-house. It is the last of the great *dagabas* to be built at Anuradhapura, and the broadest one in Ceylon. It was built by that mighty tank-builder and enemy of the

Maha Vihare sect of priests, King Mahasena in the third century. He wilfully caused it to be constructed in the Jotivana or Nandana pleasure gardens, which rightly belonged to the Maha Vihare. As it was built in the Jotivana gardens it was called Jetavanarama.

Till very recently this *dagaba* was confused with the Abhayagiri, and *vice versa*. This error which had begun as early as the time of the Polonnaruwa King, was pointed out and ably proved to be otherwise by an overwhelming pile of facts, by Mr. Parker and other pioneers.

Mr. Ievers, then Government Agent of the North-Central Province, in 1887, sunk a shaft down its axis by first tunnelling to the centre. Seven feet below the pavement a stone slab was encountered, underneath which was found a small copper coin. He reports that no relic-chamber was come across.

Mr. Bell excavated the foundations of the *dagaba* and found it to extend to twenty-six feet of brick-work, underneath which was concrete.

The belief that this *dagaba* once contained priceless treasures is borne out by the evidence of the large number of Naga reliefs which guard the *Wahalkadas* or cornices. On the east *Wahalkada* is a well executed bold pair of Naga guardians. On the same *Wahalkada* is a trace of an ancient pattern still retaining the same vivid colours of over one-thousand-five-hundred years, probably a fresco painting. (Fresco painting is the art of painting on wet plaster with colours and paints which are not affected by lime. The plaster hardens with the paint, and thereby a long life is ensured for the painting).

On the immediate east of the *dagaba* precincts are situated five of the thirteen monasteries. Between two of the monasteries there is an uncommon ruin of the same shape as the structure by the side of the Post Office. The presence of the stone 'boat' on its east aisle confirms the site as another of these *jantagharas*.

The other interesting ruin in this area is a paved structure on the immediate south of the *jantaghara*. Its general appearance and position conveys the idea that it is a *muluten-ge* or kitchen. For about a mile along Outer Circular Road no further ruins are met, till suddenly a notice board announces the Nacha Vehera. About two-hundred yards away from the road to the east, a strange ruin unlike anything else so far seen presents itself to view. It is a solid brick building of about thirty feet square and ten to twelve feet high. On the top, towards the centre, a tapering, hollow brick-built cube is to be noticed.

On three of its sides are ovoid-arch niches, there being three of them on the west. Plaster, inch thick still adheres to these niches, while in one of them traces of paint can be seen.

People believe this to be a *vehera* or *dagaba* in which the nail relics of Buddha were enshrined. Hence it was called Nacha Vehera, Nacha meaning nails.

A little further north, in private property, are faint traces of a monastery, most of the stones of which peep out from underneath nearby culverts and walls to tell the sad tale.

No more ruins are met till the grand Kuttam Pokuna or Twin Ponds comes into view. Formed of dressed slabs some ten to twenty feet long and three to four feet broad, excellently laid and most of them in perfect condition, this picturesque pair of ponds, the largest of this type of ponds at Anuradhapura, provide an imaginative example of the splendour of ancient Lanka..

Two ordinary ponds, but what artistic skill and care has been lavished in their creation!

Of the two ponds the one nearer the road had hardly a single stone displaced, till recently, an unusual shower of rain washed down the soil on one side, and the stone work slipped. Just north of the Kuttam Pokuna lies a large monastery covering a number of acres. It is of the familiar five-group, consisting of an image-house and four *awasas*, but it is a more important one than the smaller and common quincunx group as the four *awasas* are nearly surrounded by a number of quadrangular cloisters. Behind these stand an exceptional building, a shrine, with ornamentally carved stone pillars. For perfect choice of ornamentation it takes a lot to beat.

The traces of a *dagaba* and a couple of stone-lined ponds are also noticeable within the monastery precincts.

A part of an inscription unearthed close to the central image-house has been identified as belonging to Mahinda IV (tenth century). Its contents are similar to those of the Mihintale Tablets, and they give an insight into the life and administration of monasteries during the tenth century.

A whole vista of ruins nestling under the towering dignity of the Abhayagiri Dagaba close by, beckons us, but our itinerary lies along Green Path, the continuation of the Sacred Road. This is announced by a sign board which declares the distance back to the town as $1\frac{1}{3}$ miles. This road is bereft of any sacred ruins, for it passes through the ancient metropolis.

In this area interesting ancient objects are daily found. Beads probably over two-thousand years old still come to light on rainy days.

About half-way from the Kuttam Pokuna to the sacred Bo tree, on the east of Green Path, are a collection of ruins of a type seen more at Polonnaruwa than Anuradhapura.

A board announces a 'Gedige,' and branching off to the east, a complete brick structure, with solid walls twenty-five feet high still standing erect in parts, is seen. This is the only specimen of a brickwork of such magnitude and preservation at Anuradhapura, and because of its similarity to the Polonnaruwa buildings its age has been fixed as dating from the reign of Nissanka Malla in the twelfth century.

Several pots and pans were found among the debris of this ruin unquestionably disclosing that it had been a habitable building rather than a *gedige*. A startling discovery was made here when several bits of tiles were found covered with a kind of green glaze of about one-tenth of an inch thick! Was this a palace or a part of a palace? Had it any connection with Mahinda V (tenth century), who after an interval of nearly two-hundred years made Anuradhapura the capital once more? Palaces covered with tiles of green marble . . . . what dreams of eastern splendour can be conjured up. All these finds now lie at the local museum.

To the south-east of the structure an older ruin with similar bits of brick-work was recently excavated. An empty *asanaya* or sacred seat discloses where a granite Buddha had meditated in this image-house. This statue has been removed to the museum.

This building is at a lower plane than the so-called Gedige, being six or seven feet below the ground level, and for a long time lay unsuspected of its presence. It is not an improbability that there are still more ruins hidden from the 'vulgar gaze' underneath this area, awaiting excavation.

A few yards to the south of this image-house is a spacious and pillarless ruin which has been identified as the Mahapali Alms Hall, built by King Devanampiya Tissa in the third century B.C., and which was said to stand in the 'middle of the city'. The Kings who followed added to its splendour, and the *Mahawansa* further records that King Aggrabodhi I, presented it with a boat of metal to contain gruel, while his successor Aggrabodhi II, caused to be made a 'receptacle like a boat to hold rice', perhaps the very stone boat still to be seen.

To the north of Mahapali is an interesting example of an ancient well. A winding course of granite stairs leads to the water's edge in this substantially brick-walled well. Vivid pictures of fair maidens tripping lightly up the stairs with water pots balanced on their heads two-thousand years ago, spring to the imagination.

East of the well, stands a stone tablet with a very legible inscription which has been identified as belonging to Mahinda IV (tenth century). This inscription gives the identity of the multi-pillared ruin in front.

This is the Tooth Relic Palace, to which the Tooth Relic was subsequently removed from the *Dalada Maligawa* at Thuparama Dagaba, as it became the custom to have the precious relic by the King's palace. This incidentally might give a clue to the so-called Gedige standing on its north.

Back to the road, and proceeding about one hundred yards south, the site of the southern gate of the ancient metropolis is come across. For a long time this was doubted, but it was established as a fact by Mr. J. A. Balfour.

Describing the arrival of the Bo tree, the Pali *Thupawansa*, another ancient chronicle, records that they brought it by the northern gate of the city and taking it out by the southern gate, for a distance of five-hundred bow-lengths, caused it to be planted in the Maha Mega gardens.

Taking a bow-length as eight feet according to conditions then, the distance becomes 4,000 feet. Mr. Balfour measured the distance from the sacred Bo tree to the irrigation channel which was laid by Mr. Parker in 1887, and it was found to be 3,986 feet!

Mr. Parker himself believed that the low ditch in which he laid the channel was the moat surrounding the ancient city. For not more than twenty feet away is an artificial hilly ridge discernible from the road, which runs through a private garden, and is easily traceable for a very long distance. This is the ruin of the wall which surrounded the ancient metropolis.

Incidentally, a few yards outside this wall, while a well was being sunk in the compound of a Government bungalow, ten feet below the surface a few granite balls of about two inches in diameter were brought to light. One in good condition, and a broken piece are in my possession. No such objects seem to have been discovered or are be seen anywhere else at Anuradhapura. One wonders whether these were the ammunition used in the defensive artillery of the period, which the *Mahawansa* describes as, " Stones without number hurled from engines flew about from every side." With the wall of the city only some twenty yards from where these were found, this theory does not seem so improbable.

The southern gate having been definitely fixed the intriguing question arises as to where the elusive tomb of the great Tamil king Elara lies. He was killed in single combat by King Dutugemunu in the second century B.C., and the *Mahawansa* records that Elara fell near the southern gate of the city. Dutugemunu cremated the body there and built a tomb over the spot.

In the same private property, not seventy yards from the southern gate, is a gutted mound like a small ruined *dagaba*. If it had held any treasure they have long gone. But there seems to be little doubt that this is the so far undiscovered Elara's tomb, for there are no records of any *dagabas* having been built inside the actual town of Anuradhapura.

The *Mahawansa* further records that Dutugemunu made a proclamation that Elara's tomb should receive the same honours given to that of a *chakkavatti* or supreme monarch, and that all processions passing the spot should silence their instruments. How well this was observed can be judged, when in 1818 nearly one-thousand-eight-hundred years later, Pilima Talawe, the Adigar or chief minister was fleeing from the British forces, and happening to pass through Anuradhapura, though hotly pursued, yet in spite of the danger and his own fatigue, he got down from his palanquin and walked on foot for nearly a mile to be sure as he did not know the exact locality of Elara's tomb.

FOURTH EXCURSION

FROM the Bo tree junction, along Puttalam Road, past the Mirisavetiya ruins and Tisa Wewa spill, and a semi-tarred track leading to the right introduces the Outer Circular Road.

After travelling a mile along this road with only the silent jungle for companionship, a big boulder with a small dried up pond at its foot, comes into view. There are signs of an ascetic dwelling on the top of it, while on a side is seen one of those rock-cut basins which are often met with among the ruins of North-Central Province.

A little further away to the left of the road is a completely dilapidated ruin which does not seem to be of a sacred character. On the north of the ruin enclosed by a screen of stones is found an exquisite carving of a closet-stone. A short distance from the ruin is another of the same kind but of inferior workmanship.

A few yards further on, and the sight of some stone pillars peeping out of the jungle on the right, beckons us to explore them. Here is to be observed a second ruin similar to what we have already seen, but in a better state of preservation. A second and a third like ruin leads us onto a fourth splendid specimen of these buildings, and in very good repair.

Starting at a circular gateway a straight paved path of about fifty yards long led onto a guard-room. From the guard-room the path continued up to a spacious hall, which was connected with a smaller inner chamber by means of an enormous slab of granite of about twelve by fifteen feet square. The inner chamber was completely surrounded by a moat built of dressed slabs sunk into the ground. These two structures were encircled by a wide courtyard in which stood several little rooms, one on the left being invariably preserved for and easily recognized to be, a closet, by the presence of the beautifully carved closet-stone. These closets were probably for the use of the female inmates of the house, as usually another closet-stone was found outside the walls of the building.

The whole compound was now surrounded by a wall commencing from the guard-house. Outside the compound were various out-houses such as a kitchen recognizable by the broad circular mortars built into the floor, a granary, an ablution closet with its carved *kesakutiya gala*, and some distance away connected by a winding covered path, the lavatory itself. A pond completed the unit. At least four of these out-houses stood at the four corners in a beautifully symmetrical order somewhat like the five-group type of monastery.

All these exceptional buildings discovered along the Outer Circular Road are of the same pattern with little variation, and are quite unlike any other ruins found elsewhere in Ceylon. The local people call them palaces while the

Archaeological Department insists that they are monasteries.

If they had been sacred buildings it is more probable to suppose that they were nunneries rather than monasteries. But no significant sacred objects have been discovered among the precincts of these ruins, and the total absence of any carvings of Naga guard-stones and such other reliefs associated with sacred buildings, seem to justify their identity as secular habitations,—probably town residences of important ministers of the king.

These buildings must have had an imposing appearance in the time of their glory. The carvings on the closet-stones give a clue to the probable appearance they presented, and the typical eastern, artistic shape of the roofs.

From this ruin the jungle path emerges on to the Arippu Road, and continues on the opposite side to a very palatial structure of the same pattern. Here, there are no less than thirteen out-houses connected to the main building by picturesque winding paths. In one of them are still to be seen the iron sockets in which the door hinges swung. Another is attached to a bathing pond. There are no less than four closet-stones, but of simple execution. And the fanciful theory springs to the mind whether this particular lord had so much domestic trouble that he decided to allot a separate building to each of his numerous wives !

Back to Arippu Road, and following westwards the junction with Outer Circular Road is soon reached. Just north of this junction, to the left of the Outer Circular Road, a whole vista of similar ruins opens to our view. Built on a range of boulders, there are no less than three of these ruins connected with one another by paved paths. In the very first one which has been built enclosing a boulder, is to be seen a gaping square hole which according to the local residents discloses a rifled treasure trove. In the lowest of the three there is a closet-stone, a beautiful example of the stone sculptor's art now dead in Ceylon. The Sinhalese then had such an artistic sense that they could not have turned out such a common object as even a closet-stone without making it a masterpiece of sculpture.

A few yards away on the right hand side of the road, lies the least ruined of all these buildings. Some of its upper structure composing of granite slabs laid over slender stone pillars, such as the portion above the guard-room, is still in place. Several of the granite side-doors even now stand upright.

A number of artistic pillars grouped about the granite slab, connecting the inner and outer chambers, bear testimony to an exceptional sort of roof over it. Two of the pillars have capitals of a shape which are used in wood work even today.

Towards the centre of the building, connected onto the moat surrounding the inner chamber, is a delightful pond made of dressed slabs jointed together and sunk into the moat. They have a pleasing orange colour, being of a hard sand-stone. In shape it is octagonal though irregular and not one stone is out of place.

This structure even as it is, presents a vivid and picturesque sight. The local residents call it the palace of King Dutugemunu, though there is nothing to justify this assumption.

Proceeding for another few yards, two more of these singular ruins are met with on either side of the road, and then these unique specimens of ruins are left behind and no more are seen till Outer Circular Road enters the precincts of the mighty monastery of Abhayagiri Dagaba, which guarded the priests of the Vaitulya heresy.

To the south of the Outer Circular Road, and defined by the west branch of the Y Road, are a whole garden of ruins, among which three definite monasteries have been traced.

The monastery just adjoining the western pond of the two ruined ponds called the Tammattam Pokuna, composes of seven buildings, including an image-house and several residences of monks.

To the south of it is a second equally large monastery, composed of nearly twenty-one buildings. A pond on the west of it completes the unit, while a whale-like formation of rock which is referred to as Gal-ge or Rock house, forms the eastern boundary of this monastery. The third monastery occurs to the south of the Gal-ge and is in the familiar quincunx group. But the image-house of this monastery is unique in this fact that it is the only ruin at Anuradhapura to have, in addition to the pillars, two wing slabs of granite to support the roof.

Some of the stone slabs used in these buildings are over twenty feet in length, and it is a marvel to think how those sculptors of long ago managed to manipulate and fix these massive slabs without a flaw.

A pond was also attached to this monastery. On a smaller boulder lying to the west of the *dagaba* are some rough and queer carvings. There is a swastika and a couple of patterns of game boards of games which are played even today, such as Nerenchi. Another shows a swordsman of that era in a fighting attitude. Their significance cannot be explained.

South of the monastery is a large pond, while, bounding its east is a plainly traceable channel, which is believed to be an ancient channel from Abhaya Wewa.

Directly north-west of it is a large brick-scattered mound, which looks like a ruined *dagaba*. This has not been excavated.

A few yards north of the monastery is this strange whale-like rock called the Rock House. It seems to stand within a monastery of its own which included the large and picturesque Elephant Pond' on the opposite side of the Y Road.

How this pond, which is the largest of its kind among the ruins, received its name is to a certain extent explained by the porch leading to the Rock House premises, on to the parapet of which is attached a frieze of brick built elephant heads in the same manner as at Ruwanweli Seya.

On the western side of the rock is the real Rock-house. Here, towards the middle of this boulder, a slab of rock about thirty-five feet in length had been wedged off. From this had been scooped out with a perfect curve an ovolo shape. Two ledges were cut into the rock at the two corners, and the whole cave divided into three compartments. A shallow drip-ledge was also provided. This is the finest example of an artificial rock-cave at Anuradhapura.

On the top of the rock, towards the northern end, are some socket holes surrounding a smoothened area, probably the signs of a canopy over a stone bed.

On the left of the Outer Circular Road, towards the north of the Tammattam Pokuna, there are few ruins. But a continuation of the rocky backbone which runs southwards through the Rock House emerges a little beyond, and runs above the surface for some distance. On a couple of these boulders are two caves, but they are neither so picturesque nor so well executed as the one at the Rock House.

To the west of these caves there are hardly any ruins, but to the east, as far as eye could penetrate, the green glade is completely blotted out by a medley of pillared structures little damaged by road or house constructing enthusiasts, and among which several complete monasteries can be traced.

A few yards along Outer Circular Road, and a ruined solid brick structure shows the probable sight of an ancient Kovil. The local residents point this out as the place where King Dutugemunu's famous elephant, the Kadul Etha, was buried together with its pair of tusks. The king's own tomb is said to have been between the Brazen Palace and the Ruwanweli Dagaba, near the out-spreading bo tree which fringes the present playing fields along Sacred Road. That there are hardly any signs left of the monarch's tomb today is no surprise, considering the fact that an enemy would first demolish such a treasure, in order to try to get hold of the legendary wealth reputed to have been buried with him.

A little further on, a granite Buddha meditates in forest clad loneliness. Even this choice specimen of sculpture has not been spared by the vandalist, as is obvious by the cement marks of resetting plainly visible.

In front of this statue are two huge upright tablets of granite, having long inscriptions much weather worn belonging to Mahinda IV, containing rules and regulations for the conduct of the priesthood, and the scrupulous use of the lands belonging to the monasteries. They are similar to the well known ones set up by the same monarch at Mihintale.

Lying close by is another slab with an inscription of Kassyapa V (tenth century). It is a perusal of the monastic rules drawn with a view to securing the exalted prestige and purity of the Buddhist Church.

Passing the slabs, a unique but small structure comes into view. It is a beautiful granite canopy with delicate ornamentations, standing on eight slender pillars. On all four sides are splendid carvings in relief. The local resdients point this out as the place where the *Arahat* Mahinda preached to a large gathering on one of his earliest visits to Anuradhapura, and that the stone canopy was set up to commemorate the event; but there is no proof for this supposition.

Close to it is another of those charm stones with all its twenty-five chambers empty. Its presence near the stone canopy indicates that at one time this exceptional building must have housed some precious religious object.

Further on, at the elbow-bend of Outer Circular Road, a grand specimen of a stone boat unhesitatingly points out another *jantaghara* or hot water bathing place. The smaller boat lying near by with groves cut crosswise inside it, is possibly the receptacle in which the monks washed and dyed their robes. A similar *janta-ghara* is found at Mihintale too.

Leaving this behind, a majestic building with a few stone pillars of immense girth and size still standing, comes into view. From the size of its pillars it must have borne, in addition to several storeys, a ponderous and stately roof. It has a beautiful moon-stone, but of its two Naga guardian-stones only one remains.

This Naga stone is of exceptional beauty and is of a choice chocolate-orange colour, being carved out of a hard white quartz. The Naga figure is almost lifelike in its excellence of carving, and is the finest example of Naga guard-stones among these ruins.

Two closet-stones of simple execution show the situation of the lavatories. A thick brick wall separates this from the adjoining monastery. This ruin has been identified as the Ratana Prasada, the monastic palace built by King Agrabodhi VIII in the ninth century, and compared in the *Mahawansa* to a second Vejayanta, the palace of the god Sakra. It then formed the chief monk's residence of the Dhammaruci Sect.

A little beyond this is a much publicised ruin which is called the 'Queen's Palace.

King Vatta Gamani Abhaya when fleeing from the Tamils was forced to leave behind his beautiful queen Somadevi, with her own consent, so that it might lessen the weight of the chariot and enable him to escape from his foes.

She concealed herself in the Kadambappuppha forest, but was captured by a Tamil chief. When the king regained the throne and recaptured his queen, to commemorate the event, he built a monastery called the Somarama. Some believe that this ruin here, which is actually a monastery of the familiar quincunx group type, is the Somarama. In any case, this ruin is unique for the finest specimen of a moon-stone which graces the entrance to the image-house. It is a veritable masterpiece of the granite worker's art.

Among all these ruins of monks' residences, the six Uposatha Halls, and even in image-houses, a strange feature is sure to strike the careful observer. That is the corner paved stone common to all these ruins.

Several theories have been advanced to explain its significance, one of them being that it formed the platform on which stood a special image of Vishnu, kept here in a corner enclosure guarded by a screen, as is commonly seen among most *vihares* even today. Another theory advanced was that it formed a simple seat for the chief priest when teaching his pupil priests. But its exact use I think is found in the statement made in the ancient chronicles that the city of Anuradhapura, alone, had over three-thousand buildings with more than two storeys. Owing to the strict enforcement of feudalism and upholding of the caste system then, very few laymen would have been allowed to build palatial buildings with several floors. Hence most of these buildings referred to must have been religious edifices such as priests' residences. This is amply illustrated by the strength of the old foundations. Thus, these corner stones could have served no purpose other than as basements for staircares of a straight winding type,—for no slanting socket holes have been found,—or a kind of lift worked by a lever.

Leaving this ruin behind, the precincts of the Abhayagiri monastery are reached. On the left of the Outer Circular Road, to the north of the *dagaba*, is another huge monastery. A characteristic of this monastic establishment is the bulkiness of the granite work. It is a complete unit, composing of a *dagaba* and fourteen buildings, having its own kitchen and refectory. The modern vandalist has been at work here too.

To the south of this monastery lies the great *dagaba*. When King Vatta Gamani Abhaya in the first century B.C., was fleeing from the Tamils, a certain Nigantha, a Jain ascetic named Giri, jeered at him asking him why the great black *Sinhalaya* was running away. Powerless as the king was, he determined that if ever he got back to power he would demolish the Nigantha's temple and build a *dagaba* over the spot.

When the king subsequently regained his throne, he carried out his resolution and named the *dagaba*, Abhaya-after his own name,—and Giri, after the name of the Jain ascetic.

It was at the Abhayagiri Dagaba that the Vaitulya heresy found soil and grew into the powerful Dhammaruci sect, which became supreme in the reign of King Mahasena.

The nature of the relics enshrined in this *dagaba* are not known. Its height was given as 160 cubits.

In picturesqueness and dignified age it presents a sight as grand as the Jetawanarama Dagaba. But unfortunately a wall of brick is gradually creeping up, slowly but surely enveloping the *dagaba* with all its priceless archaeological treasures.

A little past Abhaygairi Dagaba, and a gorgeous granite Buddha meditates in a forest glade with an inscrutable smile hovering on the delicate lips. The eternal smile of triumph over sorrow gives a strange confidence to the thoughtful gazer, while the varying shadows seem to make the features of the Buddha change.

Between Abhayagiri Dagaba and Lankarama Dagaba is another forest of pillars which can be sorted out into several monasteries. Here too, two more of those Uposatha Halls for performing the sacerdotal rites of the priesthood, are come across.

Passing over the continuation of the ancient Abhaya Wewa Channel, the monastery of the Lankarama Dagaba is reached. This dagaba has been identified as the Sila-sobha-kandaka Cheitiya, also built by Vatta Gamani Abhaya. It is surrounded by disengaged, slender, beautiful monolithic pillars, which may have supported a roof over it. It has no basal ledges but instead this is signified by three rings of brick work. In shape it is very similar to the Thuparama Dagaba.

On its compound lie several granite Buddhas some headless and others limbless, pathetically disclosing the damage done by treasure seeking vandals. Empty holes in the remnants of the arms and heads disclose the cavities where relics and treasures had lain.

Y Road leads us back home. The only other ruin to be seen is an ancient brick built Kovil which lies by the road-side. Most probably this must have housed a Lingam and its Socket. A headless statue of a goddess found here may denote that this Kovil was sacred to the Goddess Kali.

By the bund of Abhaya Wewa now called the Basawakkulam, close to its sluice, are a sprinkling of granite pillars, or more correctly pillar stumps. This is also the site of an ancient Kovil. Now the Lingam and several other statues of Hindu Gods which the ancient Kovil once housed are placed in a mud hut,—a sad contrast from its original home.

FIFTH EXCURSION

STARTING from the Bo tree junction and travelling along the continuation of Sacred Road, the junction with Outer Circular Road soon comes into view. Here a board announces the distance to the Vijayarama as 1¾ miles, and to Asokarama as 1½ miles.

The ruins we have so far seen are all approachable by car, good motorable roads being provided. But to visit the enticing ruins to the extreme north of Anuradhapura, there is no other way but to tramp. For it is with difficulty that even a cycle could brave the deep-rutted and thorny cart track.

After passing the familiar ruins of the northern monasteries of Abhayagiri Dagaba and Twin Ponds, except for a granite slab or two to mark some ancient path, no ruins are to be found. A further mile along this road which runs through scanty forest land, and another board directs the visitor straight along to see Vijayarama, while a second points to the right directing the way to the stone bridges.

Following the Vijayarama path, and after crossing a bed of an ancient village tank, the forest which has so far been enveloping us opens out like a funnel, to disclose an enchanting glade covered with stone-pillard structures.

A pillared ruin on the southern side introduces itself as the guard-house. This gives access to a twenty-five feet wide path which stretches for nearly ninety yards. To the east of the path, close to the entrance, is a ruin of about fifty pillars with a mud floor, which was very probably the chief *awasa* or residence of the priests. A closet-stone seen in an out-house attached to this building confirms this view. Opposite the *awasa*, on the west of the path is an interesting ruin. While being excavated it disclosed signs of a fire place at one corner. The middle of the ruin is paved as among *jantagharas*. This too has been established as a *jantaghara* or hot water bath by Mr. Bell, but it is more probably the *muluten-ge* or kitchen of the monastery.

To the north of this ruin is a filled up well, lined with rough granite boulders.

At the end of the path, an imposing double entrance gateway presents four handsomely moulded pedestals on one of which is a kneeling bull in good condition. A path runs east and west of this double entrance about twenty feet wide, which is the distance between the two entrances. Towards the west end of this path the ground shows marks of several minor buildings, and the closet-stones lying about close by, give an indication to the identity of these rooms.

From the second gate of the double entrance, the path leads to the sacred precincts of the monastery enclosure proper, which is on a raised level.

On entering this holy square, a small ruined and gutted *dagaba* bares itself. Its arrangement is different and far more artistic than that of other *dagabas* at Anuradhapura, the *garbha* or bell of the *dagaba* rising from an octagonal shaped strip of a platform of shapely quartz slabs, while this in turn rose from a stone paved platform.

Vandals had broken into this *dagaba* centuries ago, but while removing the debris a few copper plates on which were engraved Pali *gathas* or religious stanzas were found. They were probably enshrined in the relic-chamber and thrown away as useless by the despoilers who broke into the *dagaba.*

From the character of the letters therein, these plaques have been identified as belonging to the tenth century. This proved to be an important discovery, as until these were found there had been no other proof forthcoming that writing on copper plates had existed in Ceylon before the fourteenth century.

The gathas when deciphered were found to belong to the *Mahayana* cult of Buddhism, thereby proving that *Mahayana* Buddhism, which is not even heard of today in Ceylon, at one time held sway.

Another interesting discovery was made while the foundations were being excavated, in the shape of several bronze images of gods and animals which were found buried at the four portals of the sacred enclosure. They were probably the guardian gods of the four directions.

With the *dagaba* there are three other image-houses, the one on the south-west corner having a headless statue of a standing Buddha.

Just below the sacred enclosure, within the path traced out by the double-entrance gateway, are ranged twelve *awasas* or residances of monks, in geometrical order, three on each side. Just outside these are a few annexes used as closets. A couple of ponds to the north and north-east respectively, complete this monastery.

But the most interesting and simultaneously puzzling piece of ruin at Vijayarama has yet to be seen. Of the four entrances to the sacred enclosure from the four directions, the one on the north gives access to an elongated hall. Four lion-head spouts drained the compound. Whether there was a roof cannot be definitely ascertained for there are no granite pillars standing in this area. Round this hall are symmetrically cut panels of granite on which are carved in shallow bas-relief some unusual carvings such as have never been seen in any other monastery. They are all of a similar pattern being single or double figures of man and woman, carved in sunk relief, within ovoid-arch niches. Over the arches are seen delicate and superb *Makara-Toranas*, (carvings of the fictitious monster Makara, adorning gateways), rivalling the one at Isurumuniya Vihare. These handsome figure carvings are connected by panels of flower patterns running round the hall.

The attitudes of the figures especially in the double-figured patterns are interesting, and instantly reminds one of the much discussed and unique panel of the male and female in a love scene, at Isurumuniya.

What connections had these carvings with Buddhism ? As at Isurumuniya was this building too, pre-Buddhist which later had been converted into a Buddhist monastery ? Or had Buddhism degenerated to such an extent at that particular period, as to include various other gods whose figures were the carvings on the panels ?

The age of Vijayarama monastery has been fixed as not later than the end of the ninth century, by the evidence of the copper plaques as well as by the measurements of the bricks used. It has not been possible to trace this monastery in the ancient chronicles, and the name 'Vijayarama' has been assumed by the local residents.

In western countries the age of ancient ruins can be ascertained by a study of their decorations and mouldings. Each decoration or carving is stamped, so to speak, with the probable age of its construction. But in Ceylon, this does not hold true. For instance, the carvings of moon-stones and Naga guard-stones found at Anuradhapura are all identical, though they may have been carved during any period from Devanampiya Tissa to Mahinda V, a range of 1,300 years.

Designs in stones such as the size and shape of socket holes of door posts, also fail to give any sure information. Hence archaeologists in Ceylon had to look out for another medium to gauge the age of ruins. And in bricks which practically litter the ruins of Anuradhapura, they found the ideal.

It was discovered that the size and volume of bricks used at a certain period noticeably differed from those of a century later, more so when the bricks were profusely used for the grander works such as the mighty *dagubas*. Thus, all that was necessary was to obtain the measurements of bricks of structures of different ages which were definitely known from records in inscriptions and chronicles, such as the Ruwanweli Dagaba, Thuparama, Abhayagiri and Jetawanarama. Then having drawn up a graph or table, it was an easy matter to read the age of any ruin, provided that the measurements of a brick from that structure were known.

Generally speaking it has been found that bricks of King Devanampiya Tissa's time in the third century B.C. have a volume of 460 cubic inches, while those used at Sigiriya in the fifth century A.D were no more than 200 cubic inches.

But again practical difficulties have arisen. It is next to impossible to come across whole bricks among ruins of such an age as those at Anuradhapura; and moreover, as most structures have been repaired at some time or other, if the age of a ruin were to be calculated on the measurements of the bricks used for the repairs, it would not necessarily be correct.

As to the first difficulty it has now been found sufficient to take only the area of a side of the bricks for the purposes of our calculations. Only great care when taking measurements can obviate the second. This system of dating has been proved to hold good to the nearest century.

Leaving Vijayarama behind, another half mile of tramping through a jungle path brings us to a grass-covered mound similar in shape to the ruin of Dakkina Dagaba on the Kurunegala Road.

The Archaeological Commissioner's efforts to excavate this *dagaba* are disclosed by two or three trenches, one alongside and one cutting in to the mound from the north. This enabled the general features of the *dagaba* to be understood. They disclosed that it was one of the oldest of the larger *dagabas* completely built of brick, but unlike others it has no stone work such as flower-alters or cornices. Another point where it differed from similar structures was that its quadrangular courtyard was laid in brick and not paved with stone.

A shaft, thirty-six feet deep was sunk through the centre of the *dagaba* by Mr. Bell.

That it had been earlier stripped of its relics and other treasures it had contained, by Tamil invaders, was proved by the gutted relic-chamber.

However at a depth of twenty-five feet, several crystalline stones and a few beads were found. Five feet lower down, a brick-built chamber was come across in which was discovered more crystalline stones, small shells and some coral. A few coins were also found at various depths.

This *dagaba* though called the Kiribat Vehera literally Milk-rice Dagaba, has not been definitely identified with any of the structures mentioned in the histories. It is also called the Menik Vehera or Gem Dagaba by the local residents. On rainy days even now pieces of coloured stones are found.

No monasteries seem to have been attached to this *dagaba*, unless they had been made of a very indurable material. But about two hundred yards to the north-east of it, a few roughly cut stone pillars standing in bleak solitude, disclose an image-house in utter disrepair Here is to be seen a piece of a giant statue of Buddha. The portion above the neck which is in fair condition measures about two feet, while the whole piece, which is only up to the waist, is about nine feet long. Now it is lying on its side, fallen from grace and badly damaged, a sad change from the lofty exalted position, the statue must have occupied in the time of Anuradhapura's glory.

To the east of the *dagaba*, a jungle path leads onto Malwatu Oya, the river that flows through Anuradhapura. Hardly any people are met along these jungle paths, and it is nothing strange to surprise a hare or two on the way.

After traversing this path for about half a mile, with the murmuring of the swirling waters getting nearer and nearer, the jungle suddenly opens out to disclose a vivid spectacle of ancient civilization,—a splendid ruin of a solid and majestic granite bridge.

It is a picturesque sight. Overhead the mighty giants of the forest successfully shut out the scorching sun thereby casting a green shade on the mossy bank. Down below, the river falls over a miniature weir of a couple of feet, into a cool pond. A fish, occasionally rising to the surface, makes a ripple go vibrating over the water. And over all, stands this ruin of the ancient bridge stretching half-way into the river, torn of all its splendour yet beautiful in its nakedness, taking our minds back twenty centuries. How many sweet maidens must have bathed in the waters below while their admirers mischievously peeped down from the bridge above. What countless processions must have passed over these very stones on their way to Mihintale. How many kings and princes must have crossed this bridge in all their pomp and pageantry.

Originally the bridge must have been about one-hundred and twenty feet long containing nineteen spans. But now, only the two spans on the left bank stand perfect; the next three have fallen, while the rest have been completely washed away.

Some two-hundred yards still further east, in thick jungle, a ruin of another granite bridge-like structure is come across. On closer examination it turns out to be a ruin of a stone dam across the Malwatu Oya, probably to turn the water into a channel now buried in impenetrable forest.

Back to the bridge, and after recrossing it, a cart-track leading south points the way to town.

Following the track for about half a mile, another ancient bridge over an old disused and silted channel is seen lying by the road side. This is in better repair. Originally it seems to have been about ninety feet long with twelve spans, but now several have fallen and have been carried away by the rush of the waters. It is a solid structure, and at one time it must have stood a good deal above the water level. But now the bed of the dried channel is only four feet below the bridge.

It is clear that these two bridges were those of a road leading north, and that the cart track follows the path of the ancient road, for just past the bridge a ruin is come across suggestive of an *ambalama* or rest-house. Further on, the occasional sight of a jutting piece of a pillar or slab confirms the idea.

This road leads straight on to the ancient village tank, Palugaswewa. A few yards north of the tank and before reaching it, a jungle path leads onto a modern brick kiln about half a mile away. And no more than two-hundred yards from this kiln, is the Asokarama monastery.

It lies on the west bank of the Malwatu Oya, and composes of thirty buildings including the ruin of a small *dagaba* in an area of about a hundred yards square. In the sacred enclosure there are four image-houses, and round this, grouped as best as the uneven ground on the bank permitted, are the residences of the monks with the out-houses attached to them. A large artificial pond with a small bund on one side, completed the monastery.

As at Vijayarama the ruins are in good condition, the granite pillars having been spared the fate of their bretheren nearer the town.

The size of the bricks found in the *dagaba* and the evidence of an inscribed pillar set up by King Mahinda IV in the tenth century, enables us to fix the age of this monastery to be about the same as Vijayarama if not slightly anterior.

But what strikes the visitor most is the absolute picturesqueness of this ruined monastery. Set in a green glade by the side of the flowing river, it has a special charm of its own. In the chief image-house is a large statue of a sedent Buddha with the right arm slightly stretched forwards, blessing the array of weeping stone pillars,—weeping for a glory gone.

During excavations several interesting finds were made, among which were two small bronze feet, one slightly larger than the other. The toes of both were turned upwards while the fingers were slightly pointed down, in the attitude of a dancer. Mr. Bell was unable to explain their presence in a Buddhist monastery. Are they perhaps the offerings of a cripple of the tom-tom beater's caste, so that he might have a sound pair of legs at least in his next birth ?

A few other limestone or chalk images of Buddha were found among the debris. They were probably offerings to the chief image, a custom which has survived to this day. These now lie at the museum.

But perhaps the most remarkable find was one of the eyes of the stone image. It was a beautiful piece of work, expertly cut from transparent crystal and stained dark blue.

As important was the discovery of two pieces of a broad silver belt inlaid with jewels, which at first sight seemed to be worth a fortune. There were emeralds, rubies, diamonds, in all some twenty-six stones. But unfortunately, the gems on closer examination turned out to be mere glass !

Of this find Mr. Bell writes: "This cannot but further confirm western opinion as to the Oriental exaggeration—to use the mildest term—of the *Mahawansa*, and like fulsome chronicles. Gem cut eyes of untold value, which more than one devoted ruler is related to have fitted to these images of the Buddha, melt into Crystal; the jewels of necklace of waist belt prove but common glass!"

But perhaps the very fact that only these spurious jems were left behind by the Tamil invaders, who deliberately sacked these sacred places, to my mind, proves that practically all the rest were precious stones which they took good care not to leave behind.

From Asokarama the road leads direct to town. Half way on the west of this path are found some ruins of Kovils, so proved by the Lingams found on the spot.

Close to these a peculiar ruin attracts our attention. It is similar in shape to an ancient *walawwa* or a nobleman's residence. However, one cannot be absolutely certain whether it is a sacred or secular building.

Some two-hundred yards away from the Twin Ponds is another of these ancient bridges, over a silted channel. Most of it is in desrepair. But what is strikingly remarkable is how well without any mortar these stones were fitted together, so that even after two-thousand years of the most scandalous neglect, that at least some spans exist in as good a condition as they were first laid.

SIXTH EXCURSION

PROCEEDING along the delightful avenue of Dickson Road, nothing of much importance is come across till a small iron bridge over an apparently dried up river, discloses the course of Halpanu Channel. A little further on, a modern bridge spans over one of the most historical rivers in the Island. It is mentioned in the ancient chronicles as the Kadamba river but is now called the Malwatu Oya.

It was close to the mouth of this river that the Sinhalese first landed in Ceylon. It was because of this river the town of Anuradhapura grew; and it was by following this same river that King Rajasingha's captive, the Englishman Robert Knox, in 1679 escaped to the coast and then to England to write his unique account of the Sinhalese Kingdom.

Dickson Road, after having crossed the railway line, leads straight up to the tank bund of Nuwara Wewa reservoir. It is one of the strangest facts but nevertheless true, that this mighty reservoir, the largest in Anuradhapura, completely escaped the notice of the ancient chroniclers.

Of all the wonderful heritage left to us by our mighty forefathers these spectacular reservoirs hold pride of place. There is no evidence to prove that tanks existed in Ceylon before the arrival of the Sinhalese, and it is very probable that these Aryans first introduced it into the Island.

No doubt that the art of reservoir building evolved gradually, beginning with tanks having small bunds and surface areas of fifty to hundred acres. Then, as the population increased and more water was needed, especially as the large supply of water required for paddy cultivation increased, bigger and bigger reservoirs were built, till finally, the most spectacular creations began to be constructed. The possibilities of reservoirs having bunds nine miles long and over fifty feet high, with water surfaces of nearly seven-thousand acres were realised in such magnificent tanks as the Padaviya. This tank which is in ruin is considered the third if not the second largest in the world even today. Writing of it Sir Henry Wood, that father of modern irrigation in Ceylon, says, that it must have taken at least fifty-thousand men working constantly for fifteen years, to construct this enormous bund.

But to make possible the creations of these gigantic tanks there was one secret principle that the earliest Sinhalese engineers had thoroughly mastered,—the secret of the sluice. Known as the Biso-Kotuwa or literally, Queen's Enclosure, it took the form of a rectangular well sunk into the bund, with granite slabs fitted with a beautiful precision and backed by mud puddle, to make it leak proof. A strongly constructed inlet underneath the bund led the water into the Biso-Kotuwa, and from it an outlet drain proceeding under the bund carried the water to the channel outside.

That this Biso-Kotuwa must have been a kind of valve-pit to regulate the flow of water seems certain, but what is surprising is that this principle was understood two-thousand-one-hundred years ago in Ceylon, while it was discovered in Europe only during the last century. So was the principle of the outlet drain. "Every engineer," writes Mr. Parker, "must feel astonishment to observe that the designer of this early sluice enlarged the sectional areas of inlet and outlet culverts from their entrance to their outlets,—a principle of engineering understood only recently in the west."

The exact means adopted in the Biso-Kotuwa is not known, for it must have been of wood work and every sign of it perished long ago. There is good ground to think that it was a simple and effective method, perhaps controlled by a kind of *welliya* or lever as is adopted in Jaffna for drawing water.

Mr. Parker continues, "I have never concealed my admiration of the engineering knowledge of the designers of the great irrigation schemes of Ceylon, and the skill with which they constructed the works."

Nuwara Wewa is one of the most scenic reservoirs to be seen at Anuradhapura. With a misty background of hills and a green forest at its water's edge, it looks like a lake from the mountains suddenly transplanted in the dry zone.

It has a water surface of 2,160 acres. This tank situated on the east side of Malwatu Oya must have at a certain period after its construction, run dry, for later, to supplement its catchment area a *Yodi Ela* or Giant Channel was constructed from the upper reaches of the Malwatu Oya to feed the tank.

As it has not been mentioned in the ancient chronicles which were written by priests, its age can be fixed only by the size of the bricks used at its sluice. This has been judged to be about the first century B.C. The local residents, however, believe this to be the original Jaya Vapi, mentioned in the *Mahawansa*. But archaeologists have identified Jaya Vapi as the pond enclosing which Tisa Wewa was constructed.

Between the railway crossing and the tank bund a metalled road leads to the north, parallel with the railway line. Along side this road lies an ancient ruin of a large monastery, popularly called the 'Toluwila Ruins', owing to its close proximity to the hamlet of Toluwila, nestling underneath the bund of Nuwara Wewa.

It is a huge monastery comprising of nearly one-hundred buildings, and is of a very unusual shape.

The sacred enclosure was situated at its northern end on a raised bank of earth. It composed of a small *dagaba* at its north-eastern end, an image-house to the south of the *dagaba*, a second image-house to the west of the first, and a Wata-da-ge or literally Circular-dagaba-house, in which at one time had been housed a miniature *dagaba*.

The *dagaba* at the north-east corner was a beautiful structure, but now sadly gutted and rifled of all its treasures. Four flower-alters grace the four directions, and a few faded flowers offered by a pious pilgrim lying on one of them brings to mind the immense harm done to these religious places by heartless vandals.

The image-house in front of this *dagaba* once housed a huge Buddha now removed to the Colombo museum. It is perhaps the finest of the larger granite Buddhas found at Anuradhapura.

The sacred quadrangle is supported by a short parapet, in the lower part of which pilasters and the head and legs of elephants in relief are noticeable. Four entrances give access to it, and surrounding these are several ruins, probably residences of the innumerable monks who dwelt here. Two artistic winding paths like the sides of a violin lead to two more pillared ruins on either side of the southern entrance, probably the residences of some of the more important priests of the monastery.

From the southern entrance of this sacred enclosure, a wide path runs directly south between two walls for about two-hundred-and-fifty yards. On either side of this central street are two rows of priest's residences separated one from another by parallel streets. Most of these *awasas* have their own out-houses and lavatories attached to them.

Half way, the street passes through a small quadrangle and a star-shaped junction, probably where the paths leading from the *awasas* outside joined the main street. Then it runs onto a large quadrangular area at its extreme south, which composes of a central terraced image-house with four *awasas* at its four corners.

The image-house is an uncommon one, being raised up by means of terraces. The only other terraced *Pilima-ge* at Anuradhapura is the one at Puliyankulama monastery, unless the mound on the west of Ruwanweli Seya near the Abhaya reservoir is another. The remnants of the artistically carved pillars show that they were of a hard lime stone. That it must have contained a sacred statue is evident by the presence of the *yantra gala* with its twenty-five chambers significantly empty. The presence of the granite *asanaya* or sacred seat, confirms this view.

The four attached priests' residences are of the kind common to the quincunx group monasteries, each having its own lavatory and out-house. The presence of the prominent corner granite slab suggests storeyed buildings. The plain *kesakutiya galas* denote where the lavatories were.

This monastery has not been definitely identified from the ancient chronicles, but the presence of bricks over three inches thick at the base of the *dagaba*, as well as the simplicity of the guard-stones denote a great age,—positively pre-Christian. The diversity of the architecture and the beauty of the carvings make this monastery one of the most interesting ruins at Anuradhapura. The local residents call this monastery the Nivatti Cheitiya, built at the spot where the *Arahat* Mahinda tarried on his first night at Anuradhapura.

Proceeding along this pleasant avenue, the junction with the Trincomalee Road is soon reached. The way then lies along the gigantic bund of Nuwara Wewa.

Nearly a mile from this junction, on the left of the road and to the north of the bund, is an archaeological reserve consisting of a piece of flat ground about one-hundred-and-fifty yards square, and surrounded by a deep moat now completely dry. At one place of the moat there seems to have been a bridge connecting the central square with some structure on the tank bund. In the centre of this moat-surrounded square are some ruins suggestive of a group of extensive buildings, but sadly despoiled of its granite-pillard upper structure.

The local residents point this out as the place where King Dutugemunu's son, Prince

Sali, built a grand palace and lived with his beautiful low-caste Chandala wife, for whom he relinquished the throne. There is no proof to support this theory.

A few yards along this road is a cross-road known as Mac Bride's Deviation, which joins the Trincomalee Road with Jaffna Road. Following this Deviation for about a mile, close to the junction with Jaffna Road, it is seen to cross over a medley of stone-pillared buildings called the Puliyankulama ruins. On examination these are found to belong to a monastery very closely following the arrangement of the buildings at the Vijayarama, but on a vaster scale.

The entrance is on the south as at the northern monastery, and a path starting at a substantial guard-house leads directly north for about ninety yards onto the sacred quadrangle. At the commencement of the path, on the east and west are two structures which look like either refectories or baths. There are four entrances to the sacred enclosure, the chief one being on the south. Inside the enclosure are a *dagaba*, sadly gutted, and three image-houses whose images and whatever other treasures that had once been deposited therein, have gone the way of all precious objects which were at Anuradhapura.

One of the image-houses bear distinct signs to show that it once sheltered a miniature *dagaba* probably built of some precious metal.

with four Buddhas placed on the four sides of it. But not a vestige of these treasures remains, while a gaping empty *yantra gala* near a second image-house discloses the sight of another treasure looted.

Surrounding this enclosure, as at Vijayarama are found twelve *awasas*. But unlike at the former, a second row of these priestly residences, five a side, stand behind the first, making in all thirty-two buildings, in addition to their lavatories and out houses. Surrounding these *awasas* which cover an area of about three-hundred yards square, is a wall of cut stones, while just outside the wall runs a deep moat. A large pond lying partly in and partly out of the monastery completed the unit.

While this monastery was being excavated, four small bronze figures were dug up at the four porches to the sacred quadrangle, but unlike at Vijayarama no animal figures were found. They were probably the guardian gods of the four directions.

This ground very possibly covers the spot where *Arahat* Mahinda first alighted on, 'in the eastern quarter of the city' and on which subsequently Patamaca or Pathama Cheitiya was built. This *dagaba* has not been identified.

When fixing the consecrated boundaries to be offered to the priesthood, Pathama Cheitiya was described as lying north-west of two special trees on the bank of the Kadamba river. Thus it appears to have been within moderate distance of the Malwatu Oya.

This river is not very far away from the Puliyankulama ruins. Could this small *dagabu*, with its monastery, now sadly despoiled of its treasures and splendour, be the sacred Pathama Cheitiya ? Even if these ruins are not so historic, the monastery here is the largest and one of the most impressive ones to be found at Anuradhapura. For symmetry of plan it has no rival.

Although to a great extent the plan of Vijayarama was followed by the Puliyankulama monastery, there was one notable exception. This was the unique hall attached to the northern entrance of the sacred enclosure at Vijayarama monastery, which is here conspicous by its absence. Instead, Puliyankulama has a feature all its own. It is a magnificent terraced image-house which lies across Mac Bride's Deviation, to the north of the pond attached to the monastery.

This Puliyankulama image-house has no rival of its class at Anuradhapura. The smaller but similar terraced image-house at the Toluvila ruins falls far short of it in size and general design. Judging from the shattered ruins of the pedestal and the solitary pillar still remaining erect, twenty-and-half feet high, Mr. Bell fixed the height of the spectacular image which must have been housed in it, as twenty-feet. Not a vestige of it remains. The grand lotus-shaped pedestal has been shattered to satisfy the loathsome greed of an unknown heartless vandal devoid of the slightest sense of the aesthetic, as a half buried empty *yantra gala* peeping out of the ground discloses.

Most of the stone pillars have been ruthlessly robbed from this building, and even the monastery has suffered the same fate. These stones now peep-out from beneath two or three unduly substantial culverts gracing Mac Bride's Deviation,—the work of road building pioneers.

To the west of the monastery, across Jaffna Road lies an extensive mound thickly strewn over with bricks, covering about three acres. This was dug into during the time of Mr. Bell, and revealed an unexpected and unusual series of structures. On a shaft being sunk into the mound, at a depth of ten feet a pavement of bricks was come across. This was gradually widened till a vertical wall was reached. On excavating along the length of the wall, it was observed to cave inwards and take an oval shape somewhat like an egg shell with its upper and lower sides cut out.

As excavations were pursued several of these shells were traced and cleared of debris. They were observed to be in a very dilapidated condition, and the utter ruin in which they were, seemed to be the work of some agency other than nature alone. The absence of any tangible discoveries other than a coin, some pieces of coloured glass and remnants of bone dust, clearly indicated that whatever objects it had contained had been rifled.

What were these queer underground shells? To what use had they been put ?

The size of the bricks denoted a great age, probably over three hundred B.C., for there were bricks that measured 15 inches by 11 inches by 3½ inches, clearly indicating a pre-Christian era. They were certainly not in any way connected with Buddhist sacred places such as monasteries. The idea of a brick kiln did not seem very probable.

Mr. Bell who excavated it suggested that it was an ancient cemetery where the bones of those cremated were deposited; and the *Mahawansa* confirmed the Archaeological Commissioner's theory.

That ancient chronicle records, that King Pandukabhaya in the fourth century B.C. constructed the 'Great Cemetery' to the west of his palace. This particular palace has not been traced, unless it be the one called Prince Sali's palace inside the moated square along Trincomalee Road, already seen. But the discovery of this cemetery provides one of the most unusual archaeological finds at Anuradhapura.

Lying along the Jaffna Road, these brick scattered rough dilapidated holes in the great ill-shaped mound do not provide a very spectacular sight. But as we think of its great age and the purpose for which it was created, as we metaphorically see, the bones of those mighty monarchs buried in state in these chambers, moving ideas fill our minds. Gone are those mighty ancestors who carved an immortal name in cold granite and spectacular gigantic embankments.

We wrench ourselves from the spot. With the Great Cemetery, we have seen the last of the immortal ruins of Anuradhapura.

SEVENTH EXCURSION

FROM the Bo tree junction we proceeded to Mihintale in a car. All the other ruins we had visited on foot, but the six miles of lonely jungle clad road is best negotiated in a motor vehicle.

Proceeding along the approach road to Mihintale which passes through a medley of ruins, where several monasteries are traceable, the foot of Mihintale hill is soon reached.

Mihintale during the time of King Devanampiya Tissa in the third century B.C., was merely a jungle-clothed hill called the Missaka mountain where the monarch used to resort to hunt deer, and most probably had been reserved as a royal deer-park. The Poson Day being a day of great festivity, the king had arranged a deer hunt, and in the course of the chase arrived at the foot of this mountain. These hunts must have been organised on a very grand scale then, for the *Mahawansa* records that forty-thousand men accompanied the monarch. At the foot of it the king suddenly espied a grazing elk, but not liking to shoot it unawares sounded his bow string; whereupon the elk fled up the Mihintale hill with the king closely following in hot pursuit.

In the meantime the *Arahat* Mahinda, the son of King Asoka of India, had arrived through the air with four other *arahats*, a *Samanera* or pupil priest, and Bhandu his nephew, and they having foreseen the arrival of the monarch at the identical mountain, were awaiting him on the top of the hill.

Devanampiya Tissa had chased the animal up to the summit, but to his chagrin, just on the point of letting fly his arrow, the animal disappeared. The *Arahat* Mahinda, who had first taken the precaution of making the other *arahats* invisible,—probably hiding them behind a tree,—for fear that the royal hunter would be frightened if suddenly confronted by such an array of strangely clad people, called the king by his name and introduced himself.

The king at first was alarmed at the sudden apparition, but on learning who the other was, took courage and advanced forward. In the meantime the others also became visible and were introduced to the king in turn.

Now the learned *Arahat* wished to test the intelligence of the king. Pointing to a mango tree close by, he asked :—" Oh king, what is this tree called ? "

" It is called a mango tree," replied the king.

" Besides this one is there any other mango tree ? "

" There are many mango trees."

" Besides this mango tree and those other mango trees, are there any other trees on earth ? "

The King was sharp enough. "There are many other trees," replied he, "but they are not mango trees."

The *Arahat* tried again.

"Then, besides the other mango trees and the trees which are not mango, is there any other ?"

But the monarch was not to be caught. "Gracious Lord," he replied, "there is this mango tree."

The *Arahat* was pleased. He questioned the king further and found that he was quite intelligent enough to understand even such a difficult philosophy as Buddhism. Thereupon he preached to the monarch and his retinue of forty-thousand, and converted them all to the new religion.

The *Arahat* made this hill his headquarters, and for forty-eight years he dwelt here in a rock cave forming the Buddhist Church in Ceylon.

Soon after he arrived in the Island, emissaries were sent to his royal father, the Emperor Asoka, and Lord Buddha's alms bowl was brought filled with relics from his cremated body. These were kept at Mihintale, and thenceforward Missaka mountain became known as Cheitiya Giri. Still later, Mihintale was known as Pabbata Cheitiya Raja.

For the convenience of the monks, King Devanampiya Tissa caused sixty-eight caves to be constructed, surrounding the future Kantaka Cheitiya, as the *Mahawansa* informs us.

After the pioneer actors in this greatest invasion of Ceylon had died, Mihintale, or Cheitiya Giri as it was then known, continued to be the most sacred fort of Buddhism, and the kings who followed vied with each other to bestow gifts and monasteries on the priest-hood at Mihintale.

From the ancient chronicles we further learn that in the course of time hundreds of *dagabas* were built on the hill, with a large number of monasteries and ponds. 1,500 granite steps were provided to ease climbing the hill, and even a hospital built for the convenience of the resident monks.

Fa Hien, a Chinese missionary who came to Ceylon in the fourth century writes :—" Forty *le* to the east of the Abhayagiri Vihare is a hill, with a *vihare* on it, called the Cheitiya, where there may be two-thousand monks. Among them there is a Sramana of great virtue, named Dharma Gupta, honoured and looked up to by all the kingdom. He has lived for more than fourty years in an apartment of stone."

With the wane of Anuradhapura's star the decline of Mihintale commenced. The lofty ideals of the religion were forgotten and even the priest-hood began to get corrupt. The degeneration was so rapid that when Mahinda IV came to the throne in the tenth century, he had to set up inscriptions in stone for the guidance of the priest-hood, with a view to re-establishing the purity of the Buddhist Church.

But the patient was dying. And this dose of oxygen enabled it to raise its head only for a short while. For, when Parakrama Bahu the Great revisited Anuradhapura in the twelfth century, it was a dense jungle. And the *Mahawansa* records that he rebuilt sixty-four *dagabas* at Mihintale alone.

As the power of the Sinhalese in the north waned and the metropolis gradually began to move southwards, the ever creeping jungle soon reclaimed its own. And it was left to the British to dig it from its woody grave and set up its bleak bones, to enable us to capture for a moment its past dazzling glory.

Just before climbing up the mountain, to the left of the great flight of steps is discernible a monastery, having the familiar quincunx group of buildings.

The Mihintale hill is about one-thousand feet high, and the ascent is facilitated by four flights of steps supposed to contain 1,500 granite slabs. On actual counting this figure has been found to be an exaggeration.

As the steps are climbed one by one, the whole hill opens out to the visitor like the enthralling sight of a virgin land to a planter's eye. Its possibilities are unfathomable.

At the top of the third flight of steps, to the left, two huge slabs of granite measuring seven feet by four feet are to be seen. These are the well known Mihintale Tablets, which have attracted so much attention from the time of their discovery, owing to the interesting account of the administration and inner life of a Buddhist monastery which they give.

It has been proved to be an inscription set up by Mahinda IV in two equal portions, for the protection of temple property.

The first portion gives the rules and regulations of the monastery, and the second part deals with the payments of servants and labourers. The rules give strict injunctions as to the payment of all work either by cash, food-stuffs or land grants; and the importance of the tablets lies in the fact that these show a true and vivid picture of a well conducted Buddhist monastery of the tenth century.

Just adjoining these tablets are the ruins of a *jantaghara*, or hot water bath, now simply called Bhojana Salawa. Two stone 'conjee boats' add further proof to the identity of the ruin.

A large picturesque pond higher up discloses the vicinity of a possible monastery. There are several ruins of stone-pillard buildings, but owing to the dense uncleared jungle closely surrounding them, it is not possible to say definitely whether they belonged to a single monastery, or were solitary buildings scattered about the hill which in itself was one huge monastery.

The fourth flight of steps leads to the summit of Mihintale, where on an evened piece of ground stands the historical Ambasthale Dagaba.

It was built by King Maha Dathika Maha Naga early in the first century, to mark the spot where the royal *Arahat*, Mahinda, stood when he first saw King Devanampiya Tissa.

Some of the relics of the *Arahat* are said to be enshrined in it. The *dagaba* was named Ambasthale after the *Amba* or mango tree underneath which the *Arahat* was seated. There is a polished stone cemented to the stone-paved courtyard, encircled by an iron railing, and this is supposed to be the very stone on which the royal monk was seated at that historic meeting.

King Dhatusena in the fifth century rebuilt the *dagaba* and conferred it on the Dhammaruci sect of priests who had got a hold on Mihintale during the time of King Mahasena. Mention is made of this sect even in the time of Mahinda IV in his tablets, clearly proving that they held parts of the hill till the very last.

The *dagaba* itself is about thirty feet high, and in many features resembles the Lankarama at Anuradhapura. It is completely built of stone and is surrounded by two rows of slender monolithic pillars which probably held a roof over it.

A broken statue on the right of the *dagaba* is said to represent the monarch's position when he first saw *Arahat* Mahinda. It is rather interesting to note that the upper portion of the body of the statue is devoid of any clothing

The base is fashioned in the shape of an expanded lotus flower and is very artistic, while the presence of three granite pillars surrounding the statue support the idea of a canopy over it.

Forming a background of towering strength, the huge granite boulder known as Aradhana Gala, literally the Rock of Invitation, rises precipitously behind the *dagaba*. Getting to the summit of the rock is an interesting climb spiced with a shade of risk. A collection box has been shrewdly placed there and no one who climbs to the top fails to put at least a cent into it, inwardly invoking the Gale Bandara or God of the Rock to guard him on the descent.

The royal *Arahat* and his party are said to have descended from their journey through the air on to the summit of this rock. And the local villagers relate that the pupil priest Bhandu, the *Arahat's* nephew, from the top of it called on the Devas or gods to come down and listen to the teachings of Buddha. Hence the name of the rock.

Coming down the Aradhana Gala, towards the left are seen shallow rock-cut steps leading up to the tottering ruins of picturesque Maha Saeya. This is one of the oldest *dagabas* in Ceylon, having been built by King Devanampiya Tissa in the third century B.C. It is supposed to contain a single hair of Lord Buddha, though not stated so in any of the ancient chronicles.

This *dagaba* is larger than the Thuparama but is different from the usual type of *dagabas* at Anuradhapura, in the fact that it has no cornices. This was also one of the *dagabas* that was rebuilt by the great Parakrama Bahu. Its final repair was done by the prisoners of Anuradhapura in the latter half of the last century, under Mr. Burrows, the first Archaeological Commissioner.

To the rear of Ambasthale Dagaba a foot path passes through some scattered granite pillars and follows a downward slope for about fifty yards; then up again onto a strangely balanced boulder called 'The Elephant Belly Rock.' The rock under the 'Belly' of the mass of stone is fashioned into a bed-like surface, well polished and raised about half an inch from the floor. It is traditionally believed that the *Arahat* Mahinda used this place as his cave. The polished surface is called the 'Bed of Mahinda.'

Back again to Ambasthale Dagaba, and exploration among the granite boulders and hills round about brings with full force the immense amount of work still to be done with regards excavation on this jungle-clothed hill.

Descending one of the four flights of steps a cleared pathway leads to the Naga Pokuna, an exquisite rock-cut pond in which is found surprisingly fresh water. On the dark rock-face, rising from the edge of the water cave fashion, is carved a huge seven-headed cobra in low relief. These five and seven-headed *nagas* are usually found carved in relief or whole near ponds and tanks or other places connected with water. Near sluices of most of the tanks it is a common sight. They are supposed to guard these places from harm.

The water from this fascinating pond is led down the hill through granite pipes some of which are still visible, and falls into a small rock-cut cistern through the mouth of a beautifuly sculptured lion's head. The tank is built on fairly level ground but on the south the ground falls sharply beneath it, on which side is carved in cold granite the full figure of a huge lion, with its forepaws in the air as if about to spring. Through the mouth of this grand lion the waste water from the tank has been made to issue. It is undoubtedly one of the finest carvings to be seen at Mihintale; though unfortunately the face is slightly damaged, yet the whole produces a highly artistic effect, which once again discloses the wonderfully developed sense of art those ancients possessed.

Passing Naga Pokuna, a jungle path points the way to the ancient Aat Vehera, literally the Distant Dagaba, on the peak of Mihintale. This is a strenuous climb but the toil is not wasted.

The *dagaba* itself is nothing very impressive being now merely a rough and ruined mound of piled up bricks. But it is worth going a long way to see the enchanting panorama suddenly unfolded before the gazer's eyes, from this peak of Nuwarakalaviya. The endless rolling seas of vivid green broken by patches of water, reflecting the heavens as if pieces of the sky had suddenly fallen down, and the little ships of hillocks all merging in the misty horizon, while towards the south, the three mighty *dagal as* of the city looking for all the world like the humps of a local Loch Ness monster, all go to provide a rare sight which cannot be easily forgotten.

This *dagaba* was probably constructed by King Wasabha in the latter part of the first century. There is little mention of it in the histories. The Mahinda Tablets however record that it was held by the Dhammaruci sect of priests.

Back again to the flight of steps, and descending a few yards, the glorious chocolate-rose *dagaba* called the Kantaka Cheitiya presents an alluring sight. Built of a hard kind of sand stone, the lower portion of it is in splendid condition. This *dagaba* bridges the gulf between the carvings of the older *dagabas* and later works such as those at Polonnaruwa. It was built in the ninth century by the beautiful queen Sena of Dapulla II, and on the whole it is one of the most beautiful ruins to be seen either at Mihintale or Anuradhapura.

Surrounding the Kantaka Cheitiya are an innumerable number of spacious rock caves with drip-ledges, and inscriptions over them.

Most of the inscriptions record that these caves were constructed at the expense of laymen and then gifted to the priesthood. The *Mahawansa* informs us that sixty-eight of these were built in the time of King Devanampiya Tissa in the third century B.C.

Descending the Mihintale hill proper, and proceeding south, a fine example of a well-planned and neatly executed monastery can be picked out. Within this is a *dagaba* commonly pointed out as the Katu Saeya and supposed to have been built by Kutta Kanna Tissa in the latter part of the first century B.C. There is a reference to this in the Mahinda Tablets in which that king is said to have repaired the 'Katu Maha Saeya.'

Passing Katu Saeya ruins, and proceeding a few yards south, a rocky hill rising steeply on the right indicate the cave-covered Raja-Giri-Lena, literally, Royal-Rock-Cave. It is fascinating to explore these deserted and bat-infested caves on the summit of this boulder. These too were probably caused by King Devanampiya Tissa along with the ones surrounding the Kantaka Cheitiya.

Down Raja-Giri-Lena, and a well worn grass track leading to the left directs the way to Kalu Diya Pokuna, or the Black Water Pond.

How this beautiful pond set in the heart of a pleasant glade got this appellation is not known. There are, however, several traditional stories in connection with it.

A ruin of an ancient *dagaba* in utter disrepair keeps sadly staring at the water from a rock on the opposite edge. Its state is no exception to the general condition of *dagabas* at Anuradhapura.

This pond forms a refreshingly picturesque sight. And it is a treat to bathe in its waters after the strenuous tour of the Mihintale ruins.

The shadows lengthen. We grudgingly rise.

And as we turn our steps back to town we cast a last farewell look at the pond. We see a fair pilgrim staring at the dark water with a puzzled look as if grappling with some mysterious problem. Perhaps it is the dim recollection of a previous birth, when she trod these very paths as a royal princess.

THE END.

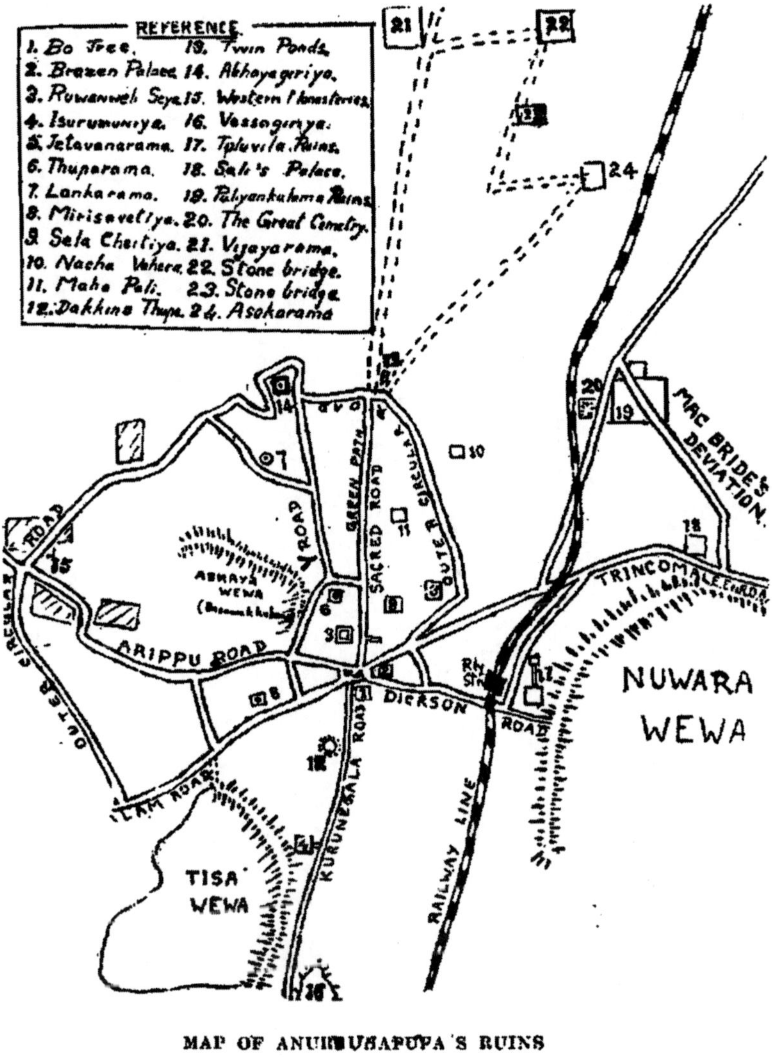

MAP OF ANURADHAPURA'S RUINS